A Last R

A Last Respect

The Roland Mathias Prize
Anthology of Contemporary
Welsh Poetry

Edited by
Glyn Mathias &
Daniel G. Williams

Seren is the book imprint of
Poetry Wales Press Ltd,
4 Derwen Road, Bridgend, Wales, CF31 1LH

www.serenbooks.com
facebook.com/SerenBooks
Twitter: @SerenBooks

ISBN: 9781781726372

A CIP record for this title is available from the British Library.

The publisher acknowledges the financial assistance
of the Books Council of Wales.

Front cover image: Chris Howes/Wild Places Photography

Printed by Severn, Gloucester

CONTENTS

Preface by Glyn Mathias   9

Jane Aaron – 'Worth the Record': A Brief Introduction
        to the Life and Work of Roland Mathias   11

The Poems

Christine Evans, from *Selected Poems* (2003)
Unseen Island   25
Casualty   26
Songline   28
Llŷn   29
Enlli   31
Off Camera   32
Case History   33

Dannie Abse, from *Running Late* (2006)
North   37
Hotel Nights   38
Iolo Morganwg   41
A Welsh Peace Offering   42
The Jeweller   44
All Things Bright and Beautiful   45
A Marriage   46

Ruth Bidgood, from *Time Being* (2009)
Viewpoint   49
Lives   52
Recovering   54
Morning   55
Letters Dancing   56
Screams   57
Porch-light   59

Gwyneth Lewis, from *Sparrow Tree* (2011)
Sparrow Tree   63
Taxonomy   64
Field Guide to Dementia   65
Guest   66
What Do Birds Say?   67
Murmuration   68

Rhian Edwards, from *Clueless Dogs* (2012)
Parents' Evening   71
Bridgend   72
Rhys   73
Outcast Hours   74
Skype   75
The Unkindness   76
Pest Controller   77

Owen Sheers – from *Pink Mist* (2013)
From 'Taff's Story'   81

Tiffany Atkinson, from *So Many Moving Parts* (2014)
Nightrunning   89
Beachcombing   90
Woman with Paperback Romance   91
Plumbing   92
Mantra   93

Philip Gross – from *Love Songs of Carbon* (2015)
I Am Those Clothes   99
A Love Song of Carbon   100
Heartland   102
Waits   104
The Shapes they Make   105

John Freeman, from *What Possessed Me* (2016)
What Possessed Me   109
My Grandfather's Hat   111
The Mug in the Common Room   112
Dannie   114
The Last Hamlet of Words   116

Robert Minhinnick, from *Diary of the Last Man* (2017)
The Body   121
Amiriya Suite   124

Ailbhe Darcy, from *Insistence* (2018)
Nice   131
Postcards from Europe   133
After My Son Was Born   136
After My Son Was Born   137

Afterword by Daniel G. Williams
Old and New Shibboleths   139

Biographical Notes   152

Acknowledgements   157

'A Last Respect' by Roland Mathias   158

Preface

This collection represents some of the best of Welsh poetry in English of this century. I can say that with some confidence because all of these poets won the all-Wales Roland Mathias Prize for poetry between 2005 and 2020. Some of them also won the Wales Book of the Year during that period, a tribute to the increasing prominence of the genre in Welsh literature.

The Prize was set up to mark the life and work of my father, who died aged 91 in 2007, as a poet, editor, literary critic and much else. It was set up under the aegis of the Brecknock Society and Museum Friends, Brecon being the Welsh market town my father lived in for more than forty years. Initially it was a stand-alone Prize for poetry and criticism staged every two years, but subsequently became the poetry award of the Wales Book of the Year run by Literature Wales on an annual basis. I owe a debt of gratitude to both these organisations. The only time the prize did not go to a poet was in 2009 when it was awarded to Jane Aaron for her study *Nineteenth-Century Women's Writing in Wales: Nation, Gender, Identity*. It is therefore fitting that she introduces the volume by way of a discussion of my father's writings. He was, as Professor Aaron notes in her introduction, 'a man of letters' of a kind less common in this more hurried age.

One of the features of the Prize was that each of the winning poets was invited to perform their work at an event in Brecon. They were all delighted to come, some of an earlier vintage recalling the help my father had given them when he was editor of the *Anglo-Welsh Review*. The performances pulled in a considerable audience and helped to enrich the cultural life of the area.

The title of this anthology, *A Last Respect*, is of course a reference to my father. It is also the title of one of my father's poems about the funeral of his father. Evan Mathias had been a minister in the Congregational church and an army chaplain for much of his career. Roland was also loyal to the Nonconformist tradition, firm in the faith, but he was a pacifist as well who had served time in prison during the Second World War. This contradiction did not affect their mutual respect. In a scene I remember myself, he describes in the poem how a breath of air 'ruffed' the flowers on the bier carrying my grandfather's body. The last lines of the poem summon up the counterpoint in their relationship:

> 'Who are you to say that my father, wily
> And old in the faith, had not in that windflash abandoned
> His fallen minister's face?'

My father would have been delighted that he had enabled this anthology of the best in Welsh poetry.

Glyn Mathias

Introduction

Jane Aaron

'Worth the Record': A Brief Introduction to the Life and Work of Roland Mathias[1]

Most readers of this book owe a debt of gratitude to Roland Mathias greater than they probably know. They may be Welsh poets writing in English or appreciators of the work of such poets; they may be students of Welsh culture or simply lovers of creative language who find something of particular interest in Welsh poetry. In each case, their debt to Mathias goes way beyond the award of a poetry prize in his name, or even the pleasure they may have derived from their acquaintance with some of his own frequently anthologized poems. Perhaps his description of Craswall on the Welsh border as a spot in which 'nightingales / Struggle with thorn-trees for the gate of Wales' recurs frequently to mind,[2] or his reference to Brechfa chapel as 'What's left of this latish day that began with love' reverberates in the memory.[3] But above and beyond such reasons for appreciation, most readers will bring with them to the perusal of these pages an awareness, however vague, of the poetry collected here as belonging to a specific body of literature which is Welsh though its language is English. And, though they may not know it, for that awareness too they owe much thanks to Roland Mathias.

Not so very long ago, within the lifetime of today's octogenarians, the leaders of Welsh cultural life rubbished the notion that what was then termed 'Anglo-Welsh' writing existed. '[T]here is not a separate literature that is Anglo-Welsh, and it is improbable that there ever can be,' argued the dramatist and founder of Plaid Cymru, Saunders Lewis, in a 1938 lecture. He based his claims on the idea that, unlike in Ireland or Scotland, the English language in Wales had never 'been the speech of an organic community' but remained the language of an alien government and educational system enforced on Wales. Consequently, '[i]t is the sensibility of the English literary body that it advances' he says of Welsh writing in English: 'Mr Dylan Thomas is obviously an equipped writer, but there is nothing hyphenated about him. He belongs to the English.'[4] Similarly Iorwerth Peate, poet and founder of the Sain Ffagan folk museum, claimed in 1936 that: 'It is idle to talk of an Anglo-Welsh literature. There is none: we have Welsh literature – and English literature by writers…[whose] work is not Anglo-Welsh in the sense that Yeats and Synge are Anglo-Irish. On the contrary, theirs is a substantial contribution to the tradition of pure English literature.'[5]

From the late 1940s onwards, Roland Mathias took upon himself the challenge of reversing such a judgement. Appointed to the post of headmaster at Pembroke Dock grammar school in 1948, he formed a local literary society and suggested that its members work together on producing a journal, initially called *Dock Leaves*. From its first number, which appeared in the autumn of 1949, *Dock Leaves* adopted 'the difficult task of pressing the right of Welshmen whose first language is English not merely to be Welshmen but to have a literary and cultural contribution to make to Wales which is something more than merely alien and English.'[6] The journal's first editor, Raymond Garlick, recruited by Mathias to the staff of the Pembroke Dock school in 1949, did much to promote that aim, for all that he was himself English by birth. It was further developed after Mathias in 1960 took over the editorship of the journal, by then renamed the *Anglo-Welsh Review*. In its pages he continued the fight for public and academic recognition for Welsh writing in English throughout the 1960s, finding but 'deserts of ignorance of Anglo-Welsh writing in the population at large, the ignorance even of graduates of English departments about their natural heritage'.[7] During the 1970s, in his Anglo-Welsh Review editorials and in other published essays, Mathias more and more pressingly advocated change in this respect, in the interest of the unity and coherent identity of Wales as a nation. In a 1973 essay on 'The Welsh Language and the English Language' he argues that 'If Wales is to remain in any sense a united society – and thereby a happy and identified society, then ... steps must be taken to associate the English-speaking majority spiritually and culturally with Wales.'[8] Welsh writers in English had as he saw it an important bridging role to play in this process, particularly given a context in which many 'of those who care what happens to Wales ... spend their energies on purely political enterprises and are insufficiently aware of the cultural poverty to which their schemes are addressed.' What was needed, as well as political and pro Welsh-language movements, was, he argues,

> a concern for monoglot English-speakers in Wales, a concern and a policy which will give them a chance to realise their Welshness somewhere else than at Cardiff Arms Park and occasionally at by-elections, which will make available through education, through bookshops, on radio and television and in newspapers, some of the riches of Welsh history and culture in English.[9]

That concern Mathias demonstrated throughout his career as an editor, essayist and cultural critic. As editor, as well as collaborating with Raymond Garlick on an anthology of *Anglo-Welsh Poetry 1489-1980*, he also supported a new generation of English-language Welsh poets in developing their craft. Robert Minhinnick, for example, one of the poets included in this anthology of prize-winners, has described how Mathias operated 'as a formative influence on his and many other poets' work ... as editor of the *Anglo-Welsh Review* for many years, he would respond to young writers and give them advice on their work.'[10] Mathias also published essay collections and monographs on twentieth-century poets like Vernon Watkins, Dylan Thomas, David Jones, Alun Lewis and R.S. Thomas, and paid what was at the time unusual attention to pre First World War Welsh writers in English. The first ten chapters of his 1987 publication *Anglo-Welsh Literature: An Illustrated History* are devoted to delineating the contribution of Welsh writers who sought to give voice in English to the needs of their country and the value of its culture from the mid-fifteenth century to the end of the nineteenth. Most of these authors had largely been forgotten, until Mathias revived their fame in essays and monographs published under his own name and in Meic Stephens' *Companion to Welsh Literature* to which he contributed a great number of entries. In general since the 1970s considerable advances have been made in the teaching of Welsh writing in English at university level; the first BA degree course in Anglo-Welsh Writing, launched at Aberystwyth in 1977, was followed in the 1980s and 1990s by further modules in Swansea, Lampeter, Bangor, Cardiff and the University of Glamorgan (as it then was). The critical recognition of Welsh writing in English as a distinct body of writing, representing one of the four nations of the United Kingdom and as such on a par with its Irish and Scottish equivalents, can by now be said to have been established. That development is in no small part due to Roland Mathias's pioneering work; he helped to create the Wales of today which for all its failings has in both of its languages a more unified sense of political and cultural identity than it had for most of the twentieth century.

But what was it that drove a history graduate, reared from four years of age outside Wales, to spend much of his adult life working to establish the distinctiveness of Welsh writing in English? The manner in which Roland Mathias explored the circumstances of his own life and sense of identity in that most personal of creative forms, poetry, provides suggestive answers to that question. In his verse apparently subjective and individual concerns constantly evoke matters of central importance to Welsh identity as a whole. Characteristically, in exploring family issues, his poems also suggest their origins and contexts within the political and cultural history of Wales, a history which of course unites both Welsh- and English-speaking

Wales. As Mathias himself once stated in an interview 'I cannot take a poetic position in which the trials of the ego are of more importance and interest than the fate of the national and cultural group to which I belong.'[11]

Take, for example, the poems by Mathias which feature his birthplace. He was born in 1915 in Ffynnon Fawr, a farmhouse situated above Tal-y-Bont-on-Usk, Breconshire, on the slopes of Glyn Collwn. But during the 1930s Glyn Collwn was flooded to provide the rapidly developing town of Newport with water. In order to preserve the purity of that water, farmers with holdings within the rainwater catchment area above the new reservoir were also dislodged, their lands taken for forestry and their old homesteads left in ruins. In a 1971 autobiographical essay, Mathias describes how Ffynnon Fawr 'stood empty for years but was pulled down in the early sixties because it had become a haunt for tramps and sheep.'[12] Ffynnon Fawr remains standing, however, as a potent symbol in many of Mathias's poems. *The Flooded Valley* was the title of both his 1960 poetry collection and a poem published earlier in *The Roses of Tretower*, his 1952 collection. *Days Enduring*, his first book of poems published in 1942, also included a poem on the flooding of Glyn Collwn. 'On Newport Reservoir' initially views the newly built reservoir from the perspective of sightseers admiring its scenic beauty. To them the few traces left of the valley's previous inhabitants, like the old railway halt at Pentir Rhiw, are blots upon that seemingly idyllic landscape:

> A pity, should a stranger say,
> That box at Pentir Rhiw that pits the face,
> The black gape of the mountain's mouth
> Forced to a cry.

It is as if the mountain itself, through that black hole, is expressing pain at its violation by the dam-builders, but the sightseer only sees the old halt as an ugly stain on the new beauty. The poet, however, who left Glyn Collwn as a child before the building of the reservoir, disagrees, saying that, on the contrary 'I…Count lovely only living as men can / The less to crave.' Beauty for him is in the pattern of life of a self-sustaining and content human community, working within nature and its seasons, rather than merely looking at it from the outside. Consequently, his response to the scene is very different:

> I pray no pardon then to mourn
> The muted line of rubble mounds beneath
> The water's level flooring, think
>   Of infant journeyings …
>   … and how …
> My father leapt the train beside that box
> And downward falling to the farm's dull life[13]
> Was happier in that force, that stain, than we
> Who silent, numerous, watch beauty's face.[14]

This is in effect a protest poem, on the enforced depopulation of a Welsh rural valley and the resultant loss of an authentic community. As such it belongs by now, since the drowning of Capel Celyn by the building of the Tryweryn reservoir in the 1960s, to an established tradition of Welsh protest poetry on flooded valleys, but 1942 is a strikingly early date for such a work. Implicit in the poem is a sense of anger at the community's impotence to prevent its demise; it can but lament the fact that its previous lived environment has been turned into a lifeless picture-postcard prettiness.

Welsh co-operating communities, 'living…the less to crave', have a significant role to play in many of Mathias's poems and short stories; however, it was initially no straightforward matter for Mathias to identify himself with such ways of life. Before his birth, in 1914, his father, Evan Mathias, had decided to contribute to the war effort by enlisting as an army chaplain, and when the war ended he took the decision to remain with the army. His children were consequently reared in Germany and then 'in various Army camps like Aldershot and Catterick which were a denial of the civilian community … Wales was the idealized distant community.' Roland's experience of Welsh communities came via visits to his cousins in the Mathias family, many of whom, despite their roots in the village of Rhos Llangeler in Carmarthenshire, had been forced by rural poverty to find work in the south Wales coalfields. 'I spent time with my cousins – in places like the Rhondda Valley, hard hit by Depression,' he recalls, 'and found them lively, generous and welcoming, despite their circumstances.'[15] Such communities were all the more appealing given that his identification with his parents' nonconformist chapel ethos, and in particular with his mother's pacifist convictions, alienated him from military camp life. During the Second World War both he and his younger brother Alun signed up as conscientious objectors, and Roland was imprisoned twice in 1941 and 1942 for insisting that not only would he not fight, he would also take no post which would free another man to fight.[16] After the war was over Mathias started to publish poetry, in part, according to his own testimony, out of a desire to connect with that 'real' community back in Wales. 'I think that the initial desire I had to write poetry about Wales', he says, 'was to celebrate some of these people who were so generous in their approach to me.'[17]

In such poems as 'They Have Not Survived', from the 1971 collection *Absalom in the Tree*, he records their struggle:

> They have not survived.
> Coughing in terraces above
> The coal, their doorsteps whitened
> And the suds of pride draining
> Away down the numbered
> Steps to the dole [...]
> For this dark cousinhood only I
> Can speak. Why am I unlike
> Them, alive and jack in office
> Shrewd among the plunderers?[18]

At its close this poem is concerned not so much with relationship as with division; through education, the poet's father, and consequently the poet himself, have risen in terms of social class, joining the ranks of the middle-class 'plunderers' while the rest of the father's family remain within the under-privileged class. Mathias presents himself as inadequate as a spokesperson for this cousinship but does not for that reason turn away from them, seeking rather for ways to bridge the distance. Personal as the poem is, this history of class division within families was, of course, a very characteristic feature of Welsh life in the first half of the twentieth century, after the introduction of compulsory free schooling and the establishment of the Welsh universities. Mathias speaks for more than one generation of 'jacks in office' who sought to reclaim their birth right through identifying with dispossessed Welsh communities and giving voice to their justifiable anger.

Nor was the relationship of his mother's family to its Welsh-ness unproblematic. While his father was 'Welsh-speaking and very conscious of the validity of Welsh culture,' his mother was reared in Ffynnon Fawr as 'a monoglot English speaker, who inherited that faint disparagement and secret hostility which was characteristic of areas which had lost the Welsh language.'[19] The poem 'Blue Blood and Englishmen' from *Snipe's Castle* (1979), focuses on Joseph Morgan, Mathias's grandfather on his mother's side, who moved to Ffynnon Fawr from Cardiff hoping to improve his health, with little knowledge of the ways of life of Welsh rural communities. When bidders at a local auction forced him to pay more for farming tools than he thought justified, he was incensed and took it as a personal attack upon him because he spoke no Welsh, without realising that such a communal manoeuvre was aimed at securing for the widows and children of deceased farmers as much profit as possible from the sale of their tools. Not appreciating this because of the linguistic and cultural division, Joseph Morgan was from then on filled with animosity against his Welsh-speaking neighbours: for him 'there was one / Offence unforgivable and he made it language'.[20] The small farming community of Glyn Collwn, vulnerable as it was to obliteration from the outside by flooding, was also torn apart by internal differences, primarily here, and indeed in the history of Wales generally since the sixteenth century, by language rather than class differ-ence. Mathias returns to the same theme in a short story entitled 'Ffynnon Fawr', in which the protagonist Rendel Morgan returns from his Australian exile to his childhood home, not only to find the farm in a half-ruined state, standing on the brink of a newly-built reservoir, but also haunted by dream echoes of bitter dissension between his ancestors and their neighbours. He consequently abandons his half-formed intention of reclaim-ing his birthplace; its present bleak and conflicted desolation is too troubling: 'He was too timid for Ffynnon Fawr, too timid to make a future where the generations cried out on him in their sleep.' And so he drives away, though '[w]hat he had been and was not and now could never be clutched at him.'[21]

The child born at Ffynnon Fawr in 1915, but early taken from it, did not however turn away from all the fraught internal differences and betrayals of colonized Wales, but rather made it his life work to rediscover his Welsh identity, understand its conflicted history, bridge its divisions, and make it unequivo-cally his own. And through his work and publications – as a poet, a short-story writer, a literary magazine editor, and a historical and literary researcher and critic – he did so not only for himself but for subsequent generations of Welsh men and women. What Roland Mathias said of the poet David Jones is also very true of himself: 'If it was no wonder that he found himself "an awful outsider", it is the more remarkable that he *felt* himself to be Welsh and felt it sufficiently to spend more and more of his life and energy in recovering for himself (and, incidentally, for others) that lost tradition of Wales.'[22] But there was nothing 'incidental' about the 'recovering for others' aspect of Mathias's work; it was part and parcel of his lifelong inten-tions, and to that life's work we, its inheritors, owe a debt worth recording.

Notes

1. The quotation is taken from the title of Roland Mathias's poem 'Not

Worth the Record', first published in *Absalom in the Tree and Other Poems* (1971), *The Collected Poems of Roland Mathias*, ed. Sam Adams (Cardiff: University of Wales Press, 2002), p. 160.

2. Roland Mathias, 'Craswall', from *The Roses of Tretower* (1952), in ibid, p. 111.

3. Mathias, 'Brechfa Chapel', from *Snipe's Castle* (1979), in ibid., p. 187.

4. Saunders Lewis, *Is there an Anglo-Welsh Literature?* (Cardiff: Guild of Graduates of the University of Wales, 1939), 13, 10, 5.

5. Iorwerth C. Peate, 'The Development of Welsh Poetry', *Transactions of the Honourable Society of Cymmrodorion* (1936), 163.

6. Roland Mathias, 'Editorial', *The Anglo-Welsh Review*, 11/27 (1961), 7.

7. Ibid., 19/44 (1971), 6.

8. Roland Mathias, 'The Welsh Language and the English Language', in *The Welsh Language Today*, ed. Meic Stephens (Llandysul: Gwasg Gomer, 1973), p. 56.

9. Ibid., p. 62.

10. Robert Minhinnick quoted in Glyn Mathias, 'The Roland Mathias Prize', *Brycheiniog: The Journal of the Brecknock Society*, 50 (2019), 16.

11. 'An Interview with Roland Mathias', in Susan Butler, ed. *Common Ground: Poets in a Welsh Landscape* (Bridgend: Poetry Wales Press, 1985), p. 184.

12. 'Roland Mathias', in Meic Stephens, ed., *Artists in Wales* (Llandysul: Gwasg Gomer, 1971), pp. 160-161.

13. i.e., 'dull' from the point of view of the tourist who has come to see scenic beauty not rural labour.

14. Roland Mathias, 'On Newport Reservoir', *Collected Poems*, pp. 80-81.

15. 'An Interview with Roland Mathias', in *Common Ground*, p. 181.

16. See Glyn Mathias, 'Roland Mathias', *Brycheiniog*, 42 (2011), 23-29, for a full account of Mathias's experiences as a conscientious objector.

17. 'Roland Mathias: An Interview', *Poetry Wales*, 18/4 (1983), 63.

18. Mathias, 'They Have Not Survived', *Collected Poems*, pp. 189-90.

19. 'An Interview with Roland Mathias' in *Common Ground*, p. 181.

20. Roland Mathias, 'Blue Blood and Englishmen', *Complete Poems*, pp. 213-4.

21. Roland Mathias, 'Ffynnon Fawr', *The Collected Short Stories of Roland Mathias*, ed. Sam Adams (Cardiff: University of Wales Press, 2001), pp. 139-141.

22. [Roland Mathias], 'Editorial', *The Anglo-Welsh Review*, 24/54 (1975), 3.

The Poems

Christine Evans

Unseen Island

From across the sleeping Sound
the unseen island
nudges at my consciousness –

wind-blown Enlli; nowhere
more steeped in calm,
more resonant of growing.

There, air trembles with associations
and I am played to a tune
I scarcely recognise

easy as water, but earthed.
Is it energy or faith
that breeds content in me?

Washed smooth, drawn out,
moulded to acceptance
like clay on a wheel,

so like a compass I am pointing
always where you lie –
elusive, shimmering –

but no mirage:
my unblurring.

Casualty

April 15, 1986, US strike on Libya

Sure it would bound back towards the green –
a wide verge thick with gorse, mist-snagged –
and my mind full of airstrikes

I did not think I noticed as the car drew level
how tall a hare can run, how easily;
staunch-thighed, a thoroughbred at exercise.

I knew the tipped alertness of its ears
and how much more presence it projected
than a rabbit, triumph in its singleness.

The long spring of its back
glowed like the ploughland I saw it swerve towards
too late. It leapt up at my wing.

Bone jarred on metal.
Fur like snowflakes in the rear-view mirror
and a suddenly-small body

belly up, offering its brightness
to the sun just breaking through.
Signalling to crows its readiness.

Gold at her throat, in the crooks
of her elbows. But truly dead
with no time to learn flinching.

Snow belly, blossom belly,
whose fruit now will not set
this morning you must signify

all peaceful browsers going quietly on
along green verges, making a dash
too suddenly, too late, for home.

Songline

for Claire Barber

Under my own apple tree
in a warm, walled garden
on an island
at the extremity of a green peninsula
in an amniotic sea

I sit and read
of nomads

so all night I hear herds
grunt and shuffle,
breathe earth and wool and leather
under a roof of antlers
on a bed of embroidered flowers.

Behind, the grasses wither.
Beyond, the passes
may be blocked with snow.
Here is sweet water, a ripening
green now. I wake

to light-filled island air
and it is so.

Llŷn

Skies tower here, and we are small.
Winters, we sleep on a flap of land
in a dark throat. We taste the salt
of its swallow. Huge cold breaths
hurtle over, cascade down
till we feel the house hunch.

When morning comes at last
houses sit up with pricked ears
on reefs of land the black tide
leaves, or sidle crab-wise
to the lane, their small squashed faces
giving nothing of their thoughts away.

In summer, flowers loosening with seed
reach out to fingerstroke
cars passing in the long sweet dusk.
Hay-meadows sigh. Pearl-pale
in the bracken on the headland
shorn ewes step delicate
and wary as young unicorns.

The sea we look out over is a navel
the wrinkled belly-button
of an older world: after dark
like busy star-systems, the lights
of Harlech, Aberystwyth, Abergwaun
wink and beckon. The sun's gone down
red as a wound behind Wicklow.
A creaking of sail away
Cernyw and Llydaw wait.

Once, here was where what mattered
happened. A small place
at the foot of cliffs of falling light;
horizons that look empty.
If we let ourselves believe it,
fringes.

V

Enlli

for Ceri when she was ten

We get to it through troughs and rainbows

flying and falling, falling and flying

rocked in an eggshell
over drowned mountain ranges.

The island swings towards us, slowly.

We slide in on an oiled keel,
step ashore with birth-wet, wind-red faces
wiping the salt from our eyes
and notice sudden, welling
quiet, and how here the breeze
lets smells of growing things
settle and grow warm, a host of presences
drowsing, their wings too fine to see.

There's a green track, lined with meadowsweet.
Stone houses, ramparts to the weather.
Small fields that run all one way
west to the sea, inviting feet
to make new paths to their own
discovered places.

After supper, lamplight
soft as the sheen of buttercups
and candle-shadow blossoms
bold on the bedroom wall.

Off Camera

It is comparisons with Eden, effusions
on the quietness of Enlli
that make them smile off camera,
the islanders returned by helicopter
to their birthplace for the day. Their faces say
this place was nothing special
more than all the hidden countries
of our childhood. The interviewer wants
hiraeth, the echoes of old loss
or an Ishmael resentment
to engage the audience and justify
his budget. But they do not seem
particularly thrilled
by the trick of sweeping back so smoothly. Even today
this white-ringed island is not inaccessible
to them; it is a real place
their minds return to regularly as the birds
to breed; the enduring pole
they measure progress from.
It is the mainland, they point out, themselves,
that have moved on.

hiraeth: Welsh, yearning for a spiritual or emotional state, or one's
country. Nostalgia.

V

Case History

There was a boy of twelve who'd never learned
To speak. Farm-bred, he had not understood
That he was more than livestock – turned
To dogs for company, came running for his food
With cats or chickens and woke with no surprise
At owls' homecoming or stars' breath on his face.
I saw him when they brought him in. His eyes
Were clear as sunlit water, held a space
We promptly crammed with language. Beyond reach
Soft wordless songs, the colours in wet stone
He loved: grass-smell; the old humanity of touch.
His brightness died, and we began to realise
Speech wakes in us so confident, so soon
What deeper dumbnesses might it disguise?

Dannie Abse

North

Between the black tree trunks
the snow, white as a frightened eye,
and still the snow-shocked road
looped North, always North.

In a stinging panic the disorder
of flying snowflakes resumed,
blown by the wind that howled
and hated us. We looked back

for our footprints but
they no longer followed;
so much blank, ruffled napery
and we seemingly anaesthetised.

The sweat froze on our foreheads
and, suddenly, we saw it
for one sublime moment only,
the white horse in the snowstorm.

Trembling, awake with otherness,
we did not shout at the wind.
Then all was as before. Silently
we tracked North again. Always North.

Hotel Nights

In the Angel Hotel

In the Angel Hotel no images allowed,
no idols. Artists, leave before midnight!

Do not strike a match in the dark laboratories
of Sleep where tomorrows are programmed.

Do not dream of stone shapes or listen to stone's
unauthorised version of silence.

Names have destinies. Write your own. Do not forge
a known sculptor's in Sleep's Visiting Book.

Else boulders will crash down. Like wood, malice of stone:
wood once took revenge on a carpenter's son.

Ignore the celestial light from the street outside,
the thud and beating of wings in the corridor.

Now read the instructions in the event of fire.
Note the nearest exit door. Sleep well.

In the Royal Hotel

Should you wake up from the usual underworld
at 3 a.m. wondering where you are, why you are,

it is fitting that you recall those adventurers
who journeyed far to meet a favoured guru.

Sheba was one such. She crossed mountain ranges,
sky-filled rivers just to hear Solomon's wisdom.

She sojourned in tents without air-conditioning,
without those other extras this hotel provides:

colour TV, Radio 2, herb-foam bath crystals,
that essential fridge stacked with refreshments.

She arrived, at last, to record his first wise words,
changed into her jewelled apparel, unaware

that three glass walls surrounded his golden throne.
And thinking shimmering reflections to be water

she raised her skirts daintily, regally approached.
Then the great king rose slowly, as if astounded.

Clutching his glittering crown with his left hand,
hesitated, then cried out, 'You have hairy legs!'

You who would seek out such sages and seers
for secret truths wrapped in obscurity, mark this.

In the Holiday Inn

After the party I returned to the hotel.
The room was too hot so I took off my coat.

It was January but I turned down the thermostat.
I took off my shirt but I was still too hot.

I opened the window, it was snowing outside.
Despite all this the air began to simmer.

The room had a pyrexia of unknown origin.
I took off my trousers, I took off my shorts.

This room was a cauldron, this room was tropical.
On the wall, the picture of willows changed

to palm trees. In the mirror I could see the desert.
I stood naked in my socks and juggled

with pomegranates. I offered offerings
that soon became burnt. This was some holiday.

I took off one sock and read the bible.
They were cremating idols, sacrificing oxen.

I could feel the heat of their fiery furnace.
I could hear those pyromaniacs chanting.

I could smell the singed wings of cherubim.
I took off the other sock and began to dance.

Like sand the carpet scalded my twinkling feet.
Steam was coming out of both my ears.

I was King David dancing before the Lord.
Outside it was snowing but inside it was Israel.

I danced six cubits this way, six cubits that.
Now at dawn I'm hotter than the spices of Sheba

What shall I do? I shall ask my wise son,
Solomon. Where are you, Solomon?

You are not yet born, you do not know
how wise you are or that I'm your father

and that I'm dancing and dancing.

Iolo Morganwg

I, Ellis Owen, antiquary and stone epitaph
    versifier,
testify this morning of February 29th, 1856,
that at Madam Totti's Wednesday night séance
widow Gweneth Jones, scrubber of germs and
    humbug
dared to ask in the tricks and shivers of
    candlelight,
'Where are you now, you rogue, Iolo Morganwg?'

What a shuffling silence! No disordered
    valediction
from the best poet ever to have languished
in Cardiff Gaol; no protesting squeak at all
from our druid-conceiver, our most loud
    tremendous liar
for whom each Bristol Channel porpoise became
    a whale;
no Welsh Red Indian curses – not a single
    scoffing word
from Iolo who faked and forged great Dafydd's
    verses
– he transcribed one, then invented seven –

until we heard his alto voice, sweet as syrup,
    saying,
'My dear Mrs Jones, my sugar lump, my hazelnut,
here I am, my old snowdrop. Here in Heaven.'

A Welsh Peace Offering

My dear felonious invective swine,
though you have often boggled me,
though I am a bard and you a mere jongleur,
I am mindful of this holy season.

I doubt if you are familiar with the story
of the two 14th-century poets,
Dafydd ap Rhys and Hywel ab Ifan
who did not wish each other well.

Dafydd scorned mead-boozed Hywel's clichés.
Hywel sneered, 'Dafydd has two duff ears.'
Each recommended the other's verses:
'A cure certain for insomnia.'

But when one was told the other had died,
by Ieuan of the drooping eyelids (ptosis),
inveterate windbag and practical joker,
both hurried home to swank their best black.

Dafydd composed a seventy-line cywydd
in honour of Hywel and the Nation's loss:
'Dead, dead, our master of the perfect metre.
Ashes, ashes, that blazing fire of a man.'

Hywel, too, played weeping harp notes in praise
of Dafydd, matchless poet, 'O how his lyrics
harmoniously soar, bible-beautiful.
An eagle's feather he did write with.'

Hoaxed terribly they were but stirred by
each other's buttered obituary
they became true friends, close as two sides
of a sandwich – as I hope we shall be.

Still I have to tell you (must be honest)
that your voice resembles an idiot tin can
animated by a relentless wind scraping
and bucketing across the road to Builth.

No matter, it's in the genes, can't be helped.
Now I send this instead of a Xmas card
confident discord between us will cease.

The Jeweller

That rainy night, the Poetry Reading over, he
    drove me home.
'As a doctor you must have seen many a bloody
    sight,
– but you poets no longer delight in the
    serenity of things.
If you had my job would you write of jewels
    fit for kings:
the delicate yellow-tinted topaz of Brazil, maybe,
or the wine-hued topaz sometimes set in
    queenly rings?'

Then I, at the traffic lights, saw the joy of
    stealthy colours
on the black wet tarmac. (First you see them,
    then you don't.)
Not the terminal jaundice in Freda's eyes, nor
    the wings
of rosacea on Goronwy's face, but the gold alloy
tiara that Clytemnestra wore at Delphi
and the heart-stopping rubies Agamemnon stole
    from Troy.

All Things Bright and Beautiful

Faint, reassuring for some, the bells outside.
This is England. Religion not quite dead!
Besides, a fat daft bee zigzagging this room
(windows open) seems to mumble a Sunday matin
and I recall how my least of religion
and my little Latin have been scrubbed out
like chalk from Brother Vincent's 6th Form
   blackboard.

Once Sir thrust his Roman beak towards me,
the bleak crucifix above his head.
'You say you never pray, boy? Never?'
All those fustian words by rote. Affluent beggars
falling to their knees in the gloom of a church
and a god in agony upon a wall.
I shambled. Was this the Inquisition?

I would not convert. Fear is the hasp of Religion.
I'd be a hero, write 'amo' in wine
and ignore the Hand no man can grasp.
Let the priest rage, kindle lightning and thunder,
thrash the cane-rod on his long black skirt.
'All I believe in, Brother, is wonder.'

And I thought of the odd idiot boy, Rhys,
on the high Wenallt range, looking down,
suddenly crying out, 'Oh, well done God.'

But now this room is quiet. The bee has
   blundered
into the garden and soon Religion's bells will
   cease.

A Marriage

Love, almost three score licit years have passed
(racist fools said our marriage would not last)
since our student days, honeysuckle nights,
when you'd open the jammed sashed window
above the dark basement flat and I, below,
would be an urgent, athletic Romeo.

Remember when I hacked my shin and swore
and you put an exclamation mark to your lips
because of the German landlady's law
NO VISITORS AFTER 10 P.M.
She kept castrating instruments for men!

Up the creaking stairs Indian file, the door
closed, you'd play before one amorous word
a Louis Armstrong record or another diverting disc
lest something of our nothings would be heard.

Oh the stealth of my burglar's exit through the
    dark,
the landlady's dog, that we called Wagner
alert, anti-Semitic, lifting its ears
to rehearse a virtuoso chilling bark.

I hear its echo still at the front garden gate,
Down the lamplit street, faint, through the
    hurrying years
to where we are, in sickness and in health,
in perdurable love, ageing together,
lagging somewhat, slowly running late.

Ruth Bidgood

V

Viewpoint

We parked the Landrover
at a rough turning-place. It had the air
not of an end but a pause
on the way through the forest.
A damp, richly green downward path
(if path it had been) was hopelessly blocked,
trunk after trunk rammed across it
like a clanging-to of bolts.
Hardly more promising, on the other side,
was a mess of boggy ruts, curving down
between banks, losing itself out of sight
below our small circle of clarity.

Feeling beyond the curve might lie
some clue to function, direction,
in the forest's enigmatic design,
we stumbled down, muddily clutching
at grass-tufts on the flanking mounds.
Suddenly, discord breaking
into harmony, we found ourselves
on a green track, surely disused for years,
but walkable, and lower down vanishing
round another curve.

I stood and caught my breath. The other two,
surer-footed, hurried on. At the bend
they stopped, stock still, every line
drawing for me their huge surprise.
Then they started to wave – "Come on!
Come! Look!", and I half-ran
the rest of the way.

The old lane twisted to a shelf of land
that opened on what might have seemed

familiar splendour – a valley we knew,
hills bare, hills forested, and far off,
beyond misty lowlands, a horizon
of true mountains. But from here
we saw it new, aslant, changed,
a beauty of questioning and strangeness.

An hour ago, across the valley,
we'd been on a known slope,
where a pile of stones could rebuild itself
into a house we remembered
from forty years ago; where bridleways
were mapped and understood,
where lines of runaway trees,
once hedgerows, delineated
fields we could trace and name;
where the man at my side
had run as a child, and today
seemed ghosted by that small shadow.

Leaning on the old Landrover
we had looked across at the hill
where now we stood, wondering
why we knew so little of it;
wondering if stones of any house might lurk
in dark of trees; how roads had run;
what meaning might be found in shapes
obscured by veils of forest.

Now in afternoon sun
we drank, delighted, the blend
of known and unknown, of our own
commingled years, of stories told
and stories waiting to be found.

I thought how the end of a life
might be a pause at the top
of a green, ancient road,
where down at the bend loved figures
would turn, amazed, gesturing
"Come! Look! Come!"

Lives

The dog dashes away again
down to the river-meadows
and disappears. We can't believe
he's lost, but pause in our snagged passage
along an overgrown path,
and call him in a desultory way.

The valley is full of life,
hardly any of it human.
Big freestanding hawthorns
are coming into bloom;
oaks, ancient vegetable presences,
sport young fern along branches,
pallid fungi on trunks.
To the top of the ridge, firs
climb close and dark. Now and then
a flick, a faint crack, break stillness.

All through the valley, in its mould,
its waters, grasses, old fallen leaves;
under its bark, stones, rushes,
carried on its winds, motes in its sunrays,
are the secret living things,
the valley's nodes and ganglions,
blood-vessels, flesh and bone –
trillions of wings, carapaces,
hairs, feathers, scales,
flakes and films of skin,
horde on horde of scuttling legs,
tiny puffs of breath, and with them
juice of leaf and stem, powder of pollen,
channelled fountaining of sap.

The terrier has found a creature to chase.
We spy him, down the riverbank,
in and out of reed-clumps.
He seems not to notice our calls,
but when we go on, taking a turn
into the trees, he pants and scurries uphill
to follow, being part (when he has to choose)
of our life, not the wild hidden one
he has wallowed in for a while.

We climb out of the valley;
our minds won't lose it.
Minute beings disrupted
by our clearing of wood from the path,
our thrusting back of brambles;
everything crushed by our trampling;
will soon be replaced by the irresistible
fecundity of the place.

Back in his home, the dog
will sleep, twitching.

Recovering

You fret at unruly speech
that won't go the way you want.
You feel you're wandering
in boggy wastes, tearing yourself
on thorns of sudden thickets.
Murky night is hiding
the marker cairn.

Sometimes I want to say
"Rest now, let dark
finish your sentence".
But then I think of how
you always dominated language,
wrenched it to shapes that held
uncompromising truth. For you,
acceptance can't be passivity.
How will you contend with this
confusion of the brain's signals?
How overcome spirit's dislocation?

At the border of your harsh new land
I wait, wishing you safe road, firm tread,
starshine, reorientation

Morning

That morning she didn't go with him
down the stairs. She heard doors
open and close, as he looked
for anything he'd left; heard
his steps in the passage –
now he'd be lifting
his old grey coat from the nail.
The latch clicked up. For a moment
came a rush of rain, till the door
shut silence in with her again.

She had meant not to look out,
but in the low-ceilinged bedroom
the small grudging window
was too available, too near. At first
there was nothing to watch, only wet trees
hiding the downward path.
Then, up the muddy track
beyond the stream, a dwindling form
climbed to the road and was gone.

Out of a shapeless pain
came the sense that to live this,
without struggle, was all she could do
to save their yesterday.
But she stood for a long time
looking at trees blowing in rain,
taking the chilly turbulence in
to her shocked mind,
wondering what it was
that might in the end be saved.

Letters Dancing

Under this picture of script on stone
the scholars' interpretation
must be taken on trust.
I'm nowhere near
fitting meaning to shape.
The letters rock and slide,
dip, reach up –
hard to imagine them
being read as words.

This is a wild alphabet
irrepressibly dancing.
It's as if Anglesey itself –
land, sea, skies, weather –
lifted and shook it,
tilted, transformed,
set something free,
according a kingly sleeper
its own eccentric homage.

Screams

In the hills, sometimes
the car-radio couldn't speak,
sometimes it stuttered out news of war.
Spared TV pictures, we still heard
enough of horror to make the day
blood-smirched. Guilt
kept us listening.
Later, the walled garden,
that archetypal enclosure,
was beautiful as ever, but today
withheld its peace.

   And then,
across artichokes and lavender,
sweet williams and raspberries,
over the head of a girl
with barrow and spade, working
moist Carmarthenshire soil,
from wall to wall, two peacocks,
one purple-green, iridescent,
the other a fantasy of white,
began to scream.

   Unhurried,
they turned their small regal heads
towards each other, antenna-crests
trembling as they opened their beaks
and sent across the garden
harsh and terrible cries.

Whatever they were expressing was not pain,
not fear, not any human thing; yet
the ugly shrieks released
into quiet air a smothered agony

that used these violent alien voices
for proxy outcry, and could then be still.

At last the peacocks were silent.
The princely white one swung his lacy tail
in a fall of courtly flounces
down the wall, and held the pose.

V

Porch-light

Years of friendship, from childhood up –
why, seven years after her death,
this trivial memory? I can't stop thinking
of her porch-light, that would spring on
if someone came to her door in hours of dark,
or lurked, slunk nearer, passed.
      When sometimes
it came on unexplained, it shone
unnervingly for half a minute, perhaps,
then switched off. "Only a cat or something,"
she'd say; I'd think "or something",
and not be reassured.
      In the isolation
of my hills I had no such device;
slept soundly, ignorant of whatever
hovered, probed, slid or padded off,
maybe returned in the black night. Here
at town's edge I sensed something to fear –
and indeed there was, for her,
but no light signalled the slow approach
of that which knew her name and habitation
and would not leave without her.

Gwyneth Lewis

Sparrow Tree

I had this tree
Where sparrows nested,
My aviary.

I welcomed a blackbird,
Which was wrong. That,
A better class of song
Went calling on the sparrows' nest.
Guess the rest.
You think I've blackbirds? They moved on
To kill elsewhere.

No tune, no subject.
Yes, imaginary birds,
But they're no use.
So, start again
With thorns, an invitation.

Taxonomy

Dusky junco, dusky junco, jay,
Towhee, testy towhee, testy towhee go
Swallow, swallow, swallow, swift,
Culture, give me cultured kite. Oh no,
The butcher bird. No! Not the shrike!
I will do, maybe, phalarope.
Ee, ah, oo, oh, oriole.

Field Guide to Dementia

To see you is egret,
No, red kite high
On a thermal,
Holding your hand
Is wagtail, comfort.

I think some cuckoo's laid
An egg of darkness in my head.

Words have migrated,
I forget their calls.

But I still point,
Look! Dowitcher, possibly
Lapwing. Quite.

Guest

A blue tit pecks at the window pane
Of your eye. It shatters, letting bird explode
In stars and auras on your retinal veins
Then up the optical nerve to your brain,
Like an idea. Painful, no doubt.
Me, I'd not want my visitor out.

What Do Birds Say?

Friday, a sparrow cried:
'Me! Me!'
That was difficult.

Saturday it was: 'You!'
I liked this no better.

On Sunday I heard
The sparrow say,
'We!' Bird and I
Enfolded together:

Syrinx, logos, feather, cry.

Murmuration

I fell among starlings,
Birds of the damned.

I understand myself to be single,
A rebel. I'm off!

They catch me,
Filing to magnetic field,
Fireless smoke.
Sighing, like electricity,
We settle in our chosen tree,
Bloody with berries.

I tell you, we had
That bush by the throat.

Rhian Edwards

Parents' Evening

We feel she may be cheating
at reading and spelling.
She has failed to grasp the planets
and the laws of science,
has proven violent in games
and fakes asthma for attention.

She is showing promise with the Odyssey,
has learned to darn starfish
and knitted a patch for the scarecrow.
She seems to enjoy measuring rain,
pretending her father is a Beatle
and insists upon your death
as the conclusion to all her stories.

Bridgend

The children are dropping like flies
in my hometown. Nineteen suicides
in no time at all. Nana would have called it
a Biblical curse. Others are guessing
it's some kind of fashion
and hanging is all the rage.
Except for the boy from B&Q,
who tied some rope to a lamppost
got into his car
and pressed down the accelerator.
A work mate found him.
He had his seat belt on,
his head had tumbled to his feet.

My father complains they only parade
the ugly side of his town.
"Why don't they show the stepping stones,
the castle or Southerndown beach?"
But then, Southerndown has been crowned
the third most popular suicide site in Britain.
Cliffs like headstones for giants!
The Samaritans have been lobbying the Vale
for years for a phone box
with a direct dial to a volunteer.
Eventually, the council surrendered and built
the box at the foot of the cliff.

Rhys

Like the time you invited me inside
the ottoman on the landing
and sat on the lid laughing
while I scratched and screamed at the wood.

Or when the babysitter wasn't looking,
you taught me the quickest way to add nine,
showed me to tie my laces with the tale
of two rabbits disappearing down a hole.

Like the day you caught the slow-worm
that tried to whip away the sun,
letting it loose into the folds
of the blanket that I held like a lover.

Not to mention the crimes I invented
for which I never knew you were beaten,
or that summer you took away the stabilisers
to be the sole witness to me riding away.

Like the times I spied in your bedroom,
played your records and fanned open your books,
only to slip between the sheets
with a nakedness meant only for bath time.

V

Outcast Hours

White light weighs heavy, bullying
bright as squash courts. I fix a dirty look
on the electric clock. The walled
minutes stagger their blinks.

Wheel-footed suitcases scurry
about me like clueless dogs,
flip flops tick-tock
on the polished rink of the concourse.

One girl's patience is vivid,
measured by the careful brush strokes
of plum on her toenails,
the soft turning of pages.

Her boyfriend hibernates,
his legs stretched out before him.
Ankles crossed, he wags his foot
conducting his concert of sleep.

A ponytailed mother raises
an eye for her wandering son.
She scoops him up and breathes in his scalp
in chase of a smell that is running away from her.

The antique couple are butchering time.
Their teeth tear through baguettes
raining faded confetti
onto their open laps.

Shy of games and companions, fidgeting
in plastic-boned chairs, we comb the air
for that splintered voice,
dictating when our sky will ship us.

Skype

For B.L.H.

Now we have fallen by way
of a window, the motion
picture of a mouth, the faithful
companion of the voice,
staggered by a split
second.

Now we can only see the other
by looking away from the lens,
the voyeur conversing
conversing with its prey,
caressing your face
with a cursor.

Now we have come to a blur,
a pixelated mashing of atoms,
stock-stilled in vignette,
we re-focus the cynosure
with the fractious waking
of a bleary eye.

Now we are a screen, a sea
apart. Three thousand miles
as the crow flies, you lean
in for the kiss with only
the blue iris of the camera
to requite it.

The Unkindness

The unkindness of flesh as it drifts
from the bone. Where the lithe
has melted into a cosy body,
plump-pillowed, an armchair for sleeping.
The skin is gathered in fistfuls,
stuffed, unemptyable pockets,
dough ripe for the kneading.
I sway the swinging bridge
of the underarm, cling to the fat
that garlands my spine.

Explain these dog-eared breasts,
the widening canyon at their root,
the browned nipple that has become
their conclusion? See these hips
scored with the Chinese burns
of dereliction and a mother's billowing.
What of this cauliflowering arse,
where are the buttocks that snake-charmed?
Riddle me this that has fallen
and lumbers in my hands.

Pest Controller

My offer of tea was cryptic code
for marriage. He politely declined,
obliging me to make small talk
about infestations. I showed him the oven,
where I accidentally roasted a mouse
and told him I drowned one in a bin
when I caught it pissing blood.

Another one came to my bedroom to die.
I explained I wrote poems to excuse
my bedlam hair, ramshackle clobber
and foul play with rodents.
What kind of stuff do you write? He asked,
sticking his head in the bathroom cupboard
while fiddling for daydreaming vermin.

Love poems, the dark side, I said
hounding him round the house, wondering
whether to give him a dedicated
copy of my book or slap on some face.
Then you don't know what love is, he said,
shaking poisoned grain into boxes
as if he were emptying a sweet jar.

Owen Sheers

from 'Taff's Story'

TAFF
It was night.
I mean Afghan night.
No lit windows. No cars. No street lights.
Just a few stars between the clouds and nothing else.
We put up lumis as often as we could –
slow-falling mortars burning bright –
but when each one came down again
so did the darkness, and with it the night.

I was on sangar duty. Half an hour left,
my eyes heavy with sleep.
It had been a bad week.
Hads had caught it just a few days before,
then my company were moved to a checkpoint
a mile from the FOB.
Right from the off things had been hot.
We were there to stir things up, draw them out,
and it didn't take long – pot shots, shoot and scoot,
RPGs finding their range.
Most days there was some kind of contact.
I won't lie, I loved it again.
Like Arthur had said in the Thekla that night,
it was doing our job. What they'd trained us for.
And a chance to pay them back,
for Hads and what they'd done to him.

A few days before it happened
a patrol came under fire.
RPGs from a compound,
hitting nearer and nearer, too close to the wire.
I was spotter for the mortars, so we went to work.
I sent them in on some smoke I'd seen,
between two trees, over a wall:

One – fell short.
Two – went wide.
Three– direct hit.
Four – to make sure.

But I was wrong. Cos Terry wasn't in there at all.
Just a farmer, his wife and their granddaughter.
Two years old, same age as Tom.
Gone.

They brought her in with shrapnel to her stomach,
a shark-fin of metal sticking out her navel.

She had burns too, all up her sides.
The medic did what he could, which wasn't enough.
She died.

We'd killed their cow too and smashed up their home,
So the liaison officer filled out the forms, paid out the bills,
and then they left.
I can still see his face, even now.
An outdoor man, skin leathered by the sun.
The way he unwrapped the end of his turban
to wipe at his eyes, raw with what we'd done.
I've wondered since if what happened next
was some kind of punishment.
But I know that isn't how it works.
That there is no one watching,
that the good lads will die, lose their limbs
while the nasty bastards go home whole.
But after I'd seen what I saw, after that,
well, you want to put some order on it all,
find a pattern, a god,
some kind of law.

ARTHUR
But you can't, can you, Taff?
Reports do that. History books do that.
But you and me, we know,
it's another word for chaos, war.
It's like they teach us:
no plan survives a contact.

TAFF
Anyway, like I said, I was on the sanger, keeping watch,
eyes heavy, when at the end of one of those lumi drops,
they attacked. Full contact, on three sides.
Small arms, RPGs, a .50 cal.

Accurate too, biting at my sandbags,
kicking up dirt from the wall.
Quick as we could we set up a defensive shoot –
flares, rockets, tracer fire.

There's a smell to battle. You learn it.
The certain tang of an RPG.
The dust and grit of an IED.
The bitter scent of your own hot gat.
The oily hint of a machine-gun belt.
But that night, suddenly,
there was something else.

LISA
'Let them have it.'
That's what the Apache pilot said.
American, called in for support.
Thought he'd found a nest of Taliban.
And he almost did,
if he hadn't been off course.

He had authorisation.
Yeah, the inquiry told us that too.
And once he did, he opened up. Blue on blue.
Chain-gun, four Hellfires and two Hydrapods.
Turning his dark screen white
as his nose-mounted sensor
traced the bodies running into the night.
Big Ash, Stevo, Lee, Tim.
And you, my love. And you.
Friendly, friendly fire.
Blue on blue.

TAFF
I was blown off the wall. Broke my back in the fall.
When I came round the first thing I saw
was a pair of plastic chairs up against a tree,
lit up by the fires, the burning tents, the flares.
Like the ones we got in the garden they were,
one blue, one green.
Just the night before, Stevo and Lee had sat in them
playing their guitars, all night long.
But all I could hear, lying there, wasn't them,
it was a dubstep song –
'Get Up' by Pinch, loud in my ears,
like I had my headphones on.
Banging away as that chopper smashed up our camp.
I stared at those two empty chairs, and as I did
the blue one started turning purple, and the green one brown.
They went hazy too, like they were going out of focus.
It was all still going down – that Apache firing off all he'd got,
but all I could hear was Pinch in my head,
and all I could watch was those two plastic chairs,
empty, lit up by the fires,
turning reddish brown and purple red.

I didn't know it at the time, but it was pink mist doing it.
Drifting across from where the first Hellfire hit.
Pink mist. Clouding my view.
That's the last I remember from that blue on blue.
Those two garden chairs, turning, then nothing.
Just a tightening of light and a heaviness of air.

        LISA
        Pink mist. That's what they call it.
        When one of your mates hasn't just bought it,
        but goes in a flash, from being there to not.
        A direct hit. An IED. An RPG stuck in the gut.
        However it happens you open your eyes
        and that's all they are.
        A fine spray of pink, a delicate mist
        as if some genie has granted a wish.
        There, and then not.
        A dirty trick you pray isn't true.
        White heat. Code red. Pink mist.
        Blue on blue on blue.

Tiffany Atkinson

Nightrunning

So much cold
even the moon can't swallow it
or the harbour in its fishy dark. You
balance your breath like a bowl of dry
ice. It's all a mistake, this body,
this job, this love. Somewhere inside
where the heart spins hard on its string
is an animal watching. It scratches
at night, perhaps with a beak or a tusk,
is neither kind nor unkind, just restless.

So much rain
even the deepest hill can't filter it
or the river with its open gills. You
carry your heart like a full dish of blood.
It's all such a blessing, this body,
this job, this love. Somewhere inside
where the lungs stretch their intricate wings
is an animal watching. It wriggles
at night and shows its belly or its tender scales,
is neither kind nor unkind, just restless.

Beachcombing

Children will enter the water hands first. There's
a knack that women all over the world have
of putting up hair in a knot, the pale nape gathers
the salt. The babushka and the magpie
own the beach but no one cares. Her fingers
strum the muscles in her thighs. She's a mountain
but her fingertips are diamonds. This patisserie
of crotches in their little wraps; how tenderly
we don't look. Airport novels crackle in the sand.
Even the baby's too dazzled to cry; his fat hands
bounce on the breeze. I have spent a half-life
on the wrong strand. Here's the barman's daughter
selling frappé. I would like a bitter chinking glassful
emptied on my head. I would like to drink the sea.
I'd like every tiny house of sand to wear me down.
When the small brown woman comes to snap the
last umbrellas shut, she'll tut and sweep the bones.

Woman with Paperback Romance

She has freed herself lately
from those hooks; her cigarette
says so and the way she snorts at each
flipped page. Let the young men detonate
across the baked sand, let them ring
the huge bell of the sea. She has the sun
for that, that keeps on, keeps on giving.
Boys, her careful wearing of dark glasses
says, get over yourselves. She balances
her backbone at the bar against a glass
of Sauvignon; in just ten days she'll land again
for rush-hour, shopping, heartbreak. What
does the dog want that howls all night,
the lizard with its soft translucent hands?

Plumbing

To your flat as high and tiny
as a needle's eye the plumber climbs
twelve flights. Nothing will drain:

the kitchen and the bathroom swill
with unsolved history. Madame
next door begins her daily tattoo

on the party wall. Meanwhile
flushing the loo three times for emphasis
he says your pipes alone drain upwards.

Well. He leaves at six to meet his girlfriend
out of Mass and fuck it every pipe
despatches straight to heaven. Oh

be careful what you wish for here;
the city downstairs is already rebuilding
itself from silverware and linen.

Mantra

The ego's a mistake
broader than Texas: you can drive
all day and still be neighbours, though
they say you shouldn't start from here

The ego's a mistake
with a finely tuned appreciation
of nicotine and Sancerre

The ego's a mistake
but an electric cockpit
nonetheless, boys, boys

    a mistake
though you marry it over and over
to your own noise

The ego's a mistake
that runs on good days twenty
hot miles on its own grease

    a mistake
in sixteen shades of lipstick
and a blonder person's dress

The ego's a mistake
like a wasp in a bottle

The ego's a mistake
with the horns and hooves
of a night truck of cattle

The ego's a mistake
that writes into the night

and puts in overtime
and talks if need be to the bloody document
and god deserves promotion

The ego's a mistake
that dances in the kitchen

The ego's a mistake
beneath the duvet after clocking-
in time still in Saturday's mascara
picking through old letters

    a mistake
flash-lit with hormone
like all creatures

The ego's a mistake
that turns up Mozart's Requiem so loud
the long-stemmed glasses in the cupboards
shake for lost friends

The ego's a mistake
that spends spends spends

The ego's a mistake
in ratios of roughly one part kiss
to four parts silence

The ego's a mistake
sharp with grievance

    a mistake
in four half-fluent languages

not including body: what a scrum –
so many moving parts

The ego's a mistake
by way of mostly false
starts

The ego's a mistake
save for itself

The ego's a mistake
hence love
hence grief

Philip Gross

I Am Those Clothes

left on the beach, folded fastidiously,
the name inside absconded.

They ran tests, but I told them nothing.
For a couple of weeks I was news.

People phoned in with their sightings
and confessions. False,

to a man, believe me.
In the end

I stood up, brushed sand from my creases
and walked, and went on walking

wondering who I could take it to,
this new and salty lightness at the core.

A Love Song of Carbon

For six years, on a high shelf in an upstairs bedroom,
　　she was the only one who did not change.

Down here, in the oxygen economy, we came and went,
　　our carbon still mixed with water, breathing, moistening,
　　　　drying – yes, even our youngest, there, etching in breath

on the glass, now a smiley or down-in-the-mouth-now
　　moon-face dripping. *He* took time, the eldest, withering

without her, needing ointments for his thinned
　　and flaking skin –– the sores on his shin did the weeping,
　　　　the chemical bonds coming loose, letting parts of him
go...

As patient as she'd learned to be in life, she
　　waited, dressed and contained – in leather-textured

cardboard round a screw-top urn. Six years till the day
　　they could meet in all simplicity, at last, entirely
　　　　conversant with each other. Ash into ash

lifts from my broadcast scatter, and into a wet wind
　　for winnowing, chalkier flakes dropping free

into wire-rooted ling, small gorse, bell heather,
　　rabbit scuts; the finer grains fetched up (we
　　　　flinch, then stay, yes, why not let them dust us)

lifting towards Sheepstor, North Hessary Tor,
　　Great Mis Tor and the deeper moor beyond

whatever skyline he and she had ever reached.
The rain clouds come up over Cornwall like the grey
Atlantic. Generations. Wave on wave on wave.

for JKG and MJAG, 10.06.12

Heartland

For each turn off a main-er
   road onto a minor, each place
     less signed, more inside itself
(the turned back
   of a corrugated shed
     its roof weighted with tyres,
three milk churns on their concrete shelf)

you could believe you're one step closer

to the heartland
   (as a loose black-and-white dog
     hurls out at your wheels) –
that the sheer lack
   of invitation is familiarity,
     as if the place could smell
belonging on you — one more blind bend,

it will shrug you in. Just one more skyline

and ... The end.
   The edge. Unkempt
     unmitigated ocean,
its botherments, its wind –
   chapped patches and spats,
     its long insistence
on telling us something it can't quite recall,

dissolved in the thin rain that's starting.

Born here, all I know
   I remember is this:
     a dimming at the window,
wind-shudder, and afterwards

drips. Drips from the low
    eaves. Slate on slate.
Beyond that, guesswork, and the weather

like a piece of elsewhere come to stay

as it did, bringing blow-ins,
    as it once brought wrecks,
        the drowned, the helped
to drown, the harvest
    of the storm; as it fell,
        leaching soil, pooling
in quarry pits, fell and then suddenly frothed

into steep streams, peat-brown, acid,

and back to the sea. Beyond
    heartland ... heart-weather,
        leaching families
out of their thin farms
    to boats, to cities, to what
        the sound of wind
had schooled them for without their knowing:

elsewhere. Somewhere to make weather of their
own.

for Mark Tredinnick, to north Cornwall

Waits

Sudden stagger-up voices
   – God, at this hour? – propped
against each other in rough harmony.
        It's not the local school,
no sign that they're a good cause
   or in any sense good news,
stumbling out of the unsilent night
        – is *that* the time
of year already? – an unholy din
   that kicks its clod boots
on your doorstep, thick with byre-
        muck and mud
from nowhere within centuries of here.

   They could injure themselves
on that rickety ladder of tune
   up to your window. Click:

the security light gets their uplifted
        faces (if
they're rosy-cheeked it's booze or bruise),
   palms out for, quick,
whatever small change you can rustle
        but too late:
they've woken the baby
   that no songs can lull,
no stories pacify ... but cries
        and cries, poor
love, all through the night, through history.

The Shapes They Make

our two bodies, together ...
and surprise us, waking

facing, in the knees-up,
chin-to-knuckle crouch

an archaeologist would recognise –

today, with hand to hand
raised, right to right,

half way between a high-five
and a handshake

like the glancing clasp of team-mates

or good rivals even, at the net,
the moment after,

the momentum still in their two bodies,
heel of hand on heel of hand, or

spent, past speaking and bent to their knees

like runners gulping air
or, emerging

on a narrow ledge at last,
at least, still roped together:

mountaineers ...

John Freeman

What Possessed Me

I cycled across London before dawn,
and as the sky paled heard a bird sing
such an echoing song I knew it must
be the nightingale Keats wrote about.
Up the terrifying dual carriageway,
with its lorries and exhaust from cars,
I kept on, one revolution of the wheel
after another, as morning became less
magic, more matter-of-fact. By afternoon
there were intervals without cars, views
over rolling green landscapes below.
I arrived at Stratford, bought a ticket,
and before the play spent shillings and pence
on a dainty meal that left me famished, angry.
I had meant to sleep in a bus-shelter,
but it was cold, and I cycled home
by moonlight, starlight, lamplight.
I found a lit blue and white machine
selling cartons of milk and as I drank
knew the pathways life was flowing
down in my arms and legs as surely
as if I could see them. At dawn
in a warm transport café my head
fell to the table-top. I was woken
with the breakfast I'd ordered,
passed out again between mouthfuls.
Round Hyde Park Corner a bus driver
gave me time and room. I never had
such courtesy from a road-user again.
I got home and looked in the mirror:
grime showing where wrinkles would be
half a lifetime later, a wild stare.

Why, said my mother, shocked.
It hadn't occurred to me to ask.
My father knew and told us. I slept
For two days, ached for a week.

My Grandfather's Hat

Most of the time I saw Granddad indoors,
first in his dark room with blue gas mantles
and a kitchen range and one tall window
in Poplar, then in the overheated lounge
of Aunt Nell and Uncle George's new flat
in Morden when he was in his nineties.
But he came to stay in our house sometimes,
and it must have been when he was leaving
that I saw him wearing his trilby hat.
It was grey and sleek like a new plush toy.
No one had ever made our two front steps
more like a staircase in a stately home,
not even Mum with her polio feet.
Crowning himself slowly, his own archbishop,
holding on to a handrail like a sceptre,
he turned with no more haste than one of the ships
he had sailed in round Cape Horn as a boy
in another century, approached each step
like a descent to be addressed with ropes.
Grandly he lowered one foot, then the other,
while we watched him, silently exclaiming
vivat, and the black and white chess-board
of the path to the front gate stretched out,
like a long drive lined with waving flags.

The Mug in the Common Room

When I need tea I go to the common room
and there's a couple who are often there.
He's always pleased to see me and he talks,
and I talk back, ask him polite questions
and, when prompted, reminisce. He's amazed
at the famous speaker I invited here –
it comes up because we've discussed his books.
I try to draw her into conversation
and get one-word answers. She might be appalled
to think she gives this impression, but the more
I talk with her friend and the happier
he seems, the more disapproving she looks.

It may be just my imagination.

Or the picture she's getting of who I am
from my stories of old times and my jokes.

My appearance.

       Dammit, my very essence
must be obnoxious to her, the more so
the more I make a prat of myself. But how
can I stop when the young man is pleased
to have an older ally in this place?

If they both had the same attitude
I'd know what to do. I would clear out fast,
or put more coins in the honesty box
and press the buttons for another tea.

As it is I drink the one I've bought, there,
instead of taking it back to my office,
and remember uneasily afterwards
that I left the cardboard mug, not quite empty,
for somebody else to tut and clear away.

Dannie

Late at night, on a screen, the news, a pang.
A year ago almost to the day he was
the last and wittiest and alas the briefest
speaker after his own birthday dinner.
That was the last time I set eyes on him.
There were many of us and where I was sitting
I couldn't say hello or shake his hand,
but when he rose to thank his well-wishers
and he looked speakingly at me, I knew
he recognised me and knew all about me
and would, as I would, have wanted to have
the conversation we had barely started.
I hoped till Sunday night we still might have it,
perhaps in the favourite London café
he wrote about in his most recent books,
or Ogmore where he lived and I take children
and friends to bathe or walk by the water.
This morning I retrieve from a high shelf
double-stacked behind more recent volumes
the old *New and Collected* and start reading,
moving between the younger and the older.
I underline a word I'll have to google.
Yes, that's one of his hall-marks, and the wit.
The doctor's and the Jew's unflinching look
into the darkness of the soul and body,
the defiant playfulness and ego,
no bones made about desire or anger,
and the spade of history and holocaust
called an unvarnished spade, though artfully.
Above all how full of energy, how full
of him his printed words are now he's stilled.
It's as if at the moment of passing
the poet's life migrates into his poems.
As he was leaving the restaurant I touched him

to hand him with a few sheepish words
a birthday card that we had written for him.
He turned with his overcoat half on
and took it with no words but such another
speaking look as beats most eloquence.
I feel his eyes on me, reading his poems.

The Last Hamlet of Words

For Carol Rhodes, painter

I went into a dozen bookshops in Hay,
that town for the cognoscenti of tomes.
I bought *The Poet's Tongue*, edited by
W H Auden and John Garrett,
another anthology edited
by Tony Frazer, and *Selected Poems*
by Ungaretti, with facing translations
by Andrew Frisardi. I nearly bought
Book Three of Ronald Duncan's five-book epic
Man, because I'd admired extracts from Book Two.
If I had seen a Roethke I'd have got it,
because of one poem of his reproduced
in Ted Hughes's *Poetry in the Making*
which I really like, though other poems
I've found by him have disappointed me.
We drove home and I nipped out again for bread
and dropped in at a charity shop and found
a thing I'd seen years before, easy to laugh
or cringe at, edited by Mary Wilson,
My Favourite Poem chosen by big names,
the poems often extracts, none with details
beyond the poet's name. Half of them I knew.
I stood there reading and glancing through, and put
the book back on the shelf and left the shop
and carried on walking around the town,
but there had been this passage by Rilke
without any clue as to where it was from.
'Exposed on the heart's mountains,' it begins, 'look,
how small there! Look, the last hamlet of words, and
higher, (but still how small!) yet one remaining
farmstead of feeling: d'you see it?' Well, I had
to have that, and when I passed the shop again

I surprised a man looking at novels
by reaching past him and removing neatly
the slim, dog-eared paperback from the pile
I'd left it on the top of. There are other things –
a de la Mare and a passage from Byron
I didn't recognise. Of course, I've got their
Complete Poems, but I shall find these things
more readily in this book. You have to be
of certain age to remember how
Private Eye mocked Mary Wilson and her verse,
what a joke she became. You don't have to
have much sophistication to see how naff
this concoction is. You have to have the nerve
to find Cinderella among the ashes,
and bear her away with you because her foot
fits the glass slipper you have always with you.
The Rilke was chosen by Prue Leith. All
royalties went to a leukaemia trust.
I paid 75p to Tenovus,
the cancer charity, on Cowbridge High Street
and went home to the hamlet of Trerhyngyll.

Robert Minhinnick

The Body

1. With the Body Piercers

There was nowhere else to sit
so I sat in the darkness with them

and listened to every word of it –
their 7 pm after work conversation.

And it seemed no different
from all the other conversations

taking place at 7 pm in the world:
that the job was thankless;

that the public was a conspiracy of fools;
that they were paid much, much too little.

And as my eyes grew used to the darkness
I understood to whom I was listening:

they were the ringed and the chained;
they were the studded and the spiked.

There were curtain hooks in their tongues;
there were amethysts in their mouths;

there were daggers through their breasts;
there were golden serpents that disappeared into their navels;

there were ingots in their ears;
there was astronomy in their noses;

there were padlocks on their eyes;
there were needles through their nipples

threaded to silver pulleys
that carried heavier and heavier silver hippopotamuses;

there were wedding rings through their foreskins;
there were swastikas in their labia.

When they had all gone
I looked at myself in the mirror:

I saw a man by himself in an empty room
tapping a pen against his teeth.

2. *The Penis*

Eye to the earth
I'm in disgrace
but point me at the stars
you'll count a constellation in my jaws.

3. *Upstairs at The Beast Within Tattoo Studio*

Ah, lover,
bend slowly over,
look for religion down on your hands and knees

and feel a mazarine blue butterfly
extinct in this country for one hundred years
alight on your right buttock.

Sister,
over your shoulder
a dolphin will bare its knuckleduster teeth.

And sir,
your torso
should be more so.
Across those plated pectorals
I'll commence my Book of Kells.

Who dares
upstairs
to the scriptorium
where Leonardo consults the hexagrams, Celtic DNA?

This needleworker
never slurs a word.
Feel his hypodermic
sip like a hummingbird.

Soon,
around town,
your children will sport his biographia.
Out of the storybooks will step your young
like little blue dragons following their dam.

Amiriya Suite

1. *After the Stealth Bomber: Umm Ghada at the Amiriya Bunker*

It is years later now
but time can also run backwards.
Still she squats in candlelight,
Umm Ghada in the caravan,
or in 125 degrees Fahrenheit,
a cockroach ticking on her divan.

At night
they come out of the bunker,
the children, the old people,
but all a fog of flesh.
One body with four hundred souls
is exposed in a photographic flash.
They pick the wedding rings and wisdom teeth
from crematorium ash.

Who was it dreamed a stealth bomber?
Stealth steals.
Think of a smart bomb.
Not so smart.
Where the missiles entered Amiriya
daylight was star-shaped in the sarcophagus,
the concrete blasted back,
all the bodies foaming like phosphorus
in a bunker in Iraq.

The old women
took off their shoes
to welcome the fire that jumped into their mouths.
How quickly their children
found themselves unborn.

Yes, stealth steals.
But still Umm Ghada
guards. Umm Ghada
who goads God
with her grief
and the ghosts she carries,
Umm Ghada my guide
in the charnel house corridors.

What is she but a woman
in desert black.
Yet no desert was ever so black
as the sackcloth that Umm Ghada owns.
Not the Syrian desert's
Bedouin black, its cairns
of cold stones.

Note: The Amiriya bunker in Baghdad was destroyed by the USAAF
on February 13, 1991. Over 400 civilians were killed. Umm Ghada,
who lost many members of her family in the destruction, became a
guide at Amiriya, living on the site.

2. WMD

We went in the convent and dug in the tomb.
There were lilyroots concealed in that sepulchure.

We halted the shepherd and looked in the mouths
of his goats. Their throats were gunbarrels.

In Babylon the computer viruses
were laughing at us all the way down Procession Street.

Within the crater of Babel
not a word was left upon a word.

In the refrigerator in the Ministry of Information.
grew a blue bacillus.

The rats in the Tigris were stoned on nerve gas
and in the market by the basilica

a farmer had written nuclear formulae
on the skin of a watermelon.

In the forbidden district
under a picture of Saddam

I peered into the hands of a beggar.
The grey dinari were pages of a book she was burning.

And believe me, I'm still looking. I am still looking.
In my mind I know exactly where they are.

3. Side Effects

Sunlight in the public bar
falls white, armorial upon him,

this Barryboy, 5'8"
in phoney CK sweatshirt,

scalp shaved to a badgerstripe,
this Blindfire chucker at Saddam.

First one in, he sits alone,
and yet there attends

anthrax at his left shoulder
whilst plague is patient upon the right:

this fatman with an empty glass
under military escort.

4. *At a Dictator's Grave*

Yes, this is what happens
when the old men make us wait.

And it crossed my mind in the cemetery
about the best way to behave:

how should I conduct myself
beside a dictator's grave?

Someone has left dandelions
in a jamjar. One o clock, two...

Yes, it's later than we think, now lover,
much later than we think.

Because this is what happens
when the old men make us wait.

Yes this is what happens
when the old men make us wait.

And it crossed my mind in the cemetery
about the best way to behave:

how should I conduct myself
beside a dictator's grave?

Why not ragwort, lover? Ivy?
Or the corpse-colour of henbane?

But crowding round, the children laugh
as children always must,

I suppose they'll still be laughing, love,
when you and I are dust.

Yes it crossed my mind in the cemetery
about the best way to behave,

but why did I not use bare hands
to dig the dictator's grave?

Because this is what happens
when the old men make us wait.

Yes this is what happens
when the old men make us wait.

I dreamed I saw our leader, lover,
as he was driven from the scene,

mottled like marble in the back
of a German limousine.

Yet all our lives we've had to drink
green water from the grave.

Yes it's later than we think, now lover,
much later than we think.

Ailbhe Darcy

Nice

Cockroaches need just
two facts about a place:

how dark
and how many cockroaches.

Or possibly just one fact,
the latter.

A cockroach was the first of us
to give birth in space.

Cockroaches can be fooled
by cockroach-scented robots

into going somewhere bright
where the mind gluts blue.

When the robot
had his mind erased

blue screen blank tape
he trampled the cockroach

but the cockroach
didn't complain.

Robots' legs are
modelled on cockroaches'.

The robot takes the scraps
we've left behind.

He squeeze-boxes
them into building blocks.

He's building a city,
an ode to the city that isn't.

Q: My son wants to know
what happened the city.

A: The summer of 2003
Europe was a fever of heat;

the old died, the young fled
the cities. I knew this girl

so we took off for Nice,
rented a room for next nothing.

What we got
was an addle of roaches.

I pulled my legs up on the chair,
cockroaches waltzing beneath.

Morning after morning,
I took off for the blue.

I swam until the city was gone,
then I floated.

Postcards from Europe

1
Our paper lanterns are not flares but sparks
off some imagined bonfire while somewhere

Europe dreams of burning, dreams of bombs
that will be sent off here and there, piercing

light, their history a history of staring
into fire. Europe dreams of burning,

dreams of bombs. A bomb is made, in part,
of light, of visits to the cinema, where Paris,

made of light, must be annihilated first.
Our lanterns are not flares but sparks.

Here the harvest's in, the children witness
to corn's absence in the field, the quince trees

stripped of all their quinces. Europe dreams of
burning, dreams of bombs. We sing and see

St Martin on his horse, a vision of the strangeness
little children swim in, beneath the light of stars.

Beneath the stars, the light of us. Our paper lanterns,
swinging as we walk, are not flares but sparks

off some imagined bonfire while somewhere
Europe dreams of burning, dreams of bombs.

2
Crossing the border between Hungary and Romania,
travelling and destination, outside and in,

was a sword swallowing act.
He was a small man on a tall stool
with feathered wings tattooed on his back.
He crowed a spiel about putting money in his hat,
shocking the children in the audience:
If a man can swallow the whole blade of a sword,
should we not fête him as the doer of feats,
pay all his bills, give him a place at court?

First you must overcome the gag reflex.
You must learn to breathe in without breathing out.
Line up the muscles of your gut,
make of your mouth a gin trap.
The thing slides in quite slowly,
take it to the hilt.
Your throat becomes the rut for the runners of a sleigh,
your tonsils lean to lick at it,
the metal of your fillings sings,
your tongue tastes the cold, a long, cold drink.
Fillings singing like blades in a drawer, the train entering a
    tunnel,
things that go where they belong, belong where they are,
a carp's scale in a shepherd's purse,
the sword is gone.

Children wonder at the trick.
They wonder that an adult hasn't clapped hands over their
    eyes,
sent them to bed.
They wonder at the man passing round a hat, what it will
    take
to make their lives heroic.
The border police came and went.
The train was like the Orient Express

134

and we shared our compartment with a Romanian
coming home from a student union meeting in Prague.

3
Beneath the floating railway
the ghosts of horses sweat light.
They were to be, they were never to be.
How they swam the length
of the Wupper in the conditional
we'll never know.
                    One day the monorail
will give birth to an elephant, a perfect execution
docked for want of a springboard.
Recall the unfair decision, a half-century
earlier, to value grace and ease
over difficult failure
in plunging forth.
                    Emperor Wilhelm II,
palsy akimbo, will ace his own stunt
on the Schwebebahn, who years before
chomped the leg of Uncle Alfred
Duke of Edinburgh,
as Edison chomped the phonograph.
No doubt to sink a hold on these vibrations
that issue constantly forth
and constantly fold back on us.
                    Suspended above Wuppertal,
swooping left and right,
how we might holler, spared the breath for it!
How we might insist on going around again,
on none of this business of history
having anything to do with itself.

After my son was born

I'd a snip cut in his tongue.
Blood scissored down his chin.
At every squall I'd been unsnibbing
myself and starving him. He knocked
me so my nose coughed blood,
punched a finger through my cornea.
Blood blubbed on my nipple
where his gums met. On the radio
somebody was saying something about Syria.
My son jerked knots of hair from my head,
tears dashed off his fontanelle. He'd fixed
my hips so my clothes didn't fit. I blundered
him once against the door-jamb:
blood. I'd bit his father
when we were younger, drinking harder,
made blood come then. Twice I tried to leave
him screaming, twenty minutes at a time,
but couldn't keep schtum.
One breakfast I broke the mug that insisted
'Don't Mess With Texas.'
Smashed it. And all the time
I smiled so much my teeth dried.
He made everything heavy.
Like they say the bomb did for a while,
that Americans swam
through their homes, eyes peeled,
picking up everyday things and dropping them
as though they were violated with light and pain.
As though blood hadn't always been there, waiting.

After my son was born

grit shone on the surfaces
of my bedazzled eyes.

Flesh pooled about me,
so that it was difficult to run.

Disease squeaked an entrance
at the corners of window frames,
the gap beneath the door, my
shut mouth.

I wished you all dead.

After my son was born,
my mother came to me
and was gentle.

Afterword: Old and New Shibboleths
Daniel G. Williams

I

Towards the conclusion of his *Anglo-Welsh Literature: An Illustrated History*, Roland Mathias speaks of shibboleths:

> Some of the youthful energy that might have gone into writing in English in the highly populated districts has been turned towards the learning of the Welsh language and there is a widespread attempt to create a strictly modern 'Welshness' which ignores old shibboleths like the values of Nonconformity and the closeness of the rural community. This new situation leaves the young writer who, for whatever reason, has not chosen to opt into Welsh, more separated from 'Welshness' than his predecessors were because the shibboleth is now almost solely that of the language. Not having that, he is much more completely shut out from the Welsh world than if there were, as there once was, a recognisably different lifestyle to attract him.[1]

'Shibboleth' is an interesting word. It is distinct from almost all others in that its original meaning in Hebrew ('ear of corn' or 'stream') differs from its meaning in English ('secret test word' or 'social discriminator'). For English speakers the meaning of 'shibboleth' derives not from what it means in Hebrew, but from its function in the Old Testament's 'Book of Judges'. In The Bible, the word describes a method for distinguishing foreign speakers from native speakers, and thus for deciding who to kill:

> 5. And the Gileadites took the passages of Jordan before the Ephraimites: and it was so, that when those Ephraimites which were escaped said, Let me go over; that the men of

Gilead said unto him, *Art* thou an Ephraimite? If he said ,
Nay;
6. Then said they unto him, Say now Shibboleth: and he said
Sibboleth: for he could not frame to pronounce it right. Then
they took him, and slew him at the passages of Jordan: and
there fell at that time of the Ephraimites forty and two
thousand.[2]

The assumption here is that all members of my tribe are able to
pronounce the 'sh' sound, while those who are not members of
my tribe cannot pronounce the 'sh' sound and utter 's' in its
place. From one perspective the shibboleth is a social discriminator and boundary marker. From another it is the gateway into
a culture, a signifier of belonging. In both readings, it is a matter
of life and death.[3]

These contradictory meanings seem to inform Roland
Mathias's use of the term above. It would seem that shibboleths
were important to a critic who – as Jane Aaron notes in her
introductory essay – despite being educated at a series of British
military schools in Germany and spending much of his working
life teaching in Derbyshire, dedicated his critical work to
excavating and understanding the Anglophone literature of
Wales. As Mathias pays 'A Last Respect' to his father in the
poem that gives this anthology its title, do we not detect an echo
of the linguistic divisions of the 'Book of Judges' as the 'gutteral
base' of the hearse travelling towards 'the pinnacles / Of Sion'
resonates with the Welsh-speaking minister's 'last thick syllables' that 'dissuade the tongue' of the son who is an
Anglophone critic and poet?[4] The danger alluded to in the
poem and made explicit in the conclusion to *An Illustrated
History* is that the cultural prestige and pre-eminence accorded
to the Welsh language dissuades non-Welsh-speakers from
identifying with the tribe. They remain on the wrong side of the
river.

Mathias's deployment of the word shibboleth to express his
fear that the 'Anglo-Welsh' may find themselves 'completely
shut out from the Welsh world', challenges an influential

reading of Welsh culture. Many creative writers and critics, across several decades if not centuries, have sensed that the experience of 'writing on the edge', on the precipice of cultural obsolescence, is a characteristic of the Welsh condition.[5] That argument is predominantly articulated in relation to the Welsh language. As Jane Aaron notes in the introduction, in the 1930s Saunders Lewis and Iorwerth Peate viewed the English language itself as a threat to a Welsh identity defined in linguistic terms, and responded to the rise of Anglo-Welsh literature by denying its hybrid status, viewing it as wholly English and its authors as 'belong[ing] to the English'.[6] In the 1960s and 70s the philosopher J.R. Jones influenced those fighting for Welsh linguistic rights with his argument that 'an equally desperate experience' to that of being forced into exile is

> the experience of knowing, not that you are leaving your nation, but that your nation is leaving you, disappearing beneath your feet, being sucked away around you, as if by a ravenous tornado, into the hands and ownership of another nation and civilization.[7]

J.R. Jones is speaking of the Anglicisation of Wales, and the breaking of that valuable inter-penetration (*cydymdreiddiad*) of language and territory which he felt was crucial for sustaining a separate national identity. The terms of Roland Mathias's conclusion are slightly less dramatic, though the Biblical resonances suggest that he is also engaging with the roots of identity and the boundaries of cultural difference. In Mathias's reading, interventions such as those offered by Lewis, Peate and Jones regarding the centrality of the Welsh language, and the movements inspired by them, were not reinforcing but were actually threatening the 'older' non-linguistic shibboleths – 'the values of Nonconformity and the closeness of the rural community' – which marked the boundaries of, while also allowing entry-points into, Welshness. The result was that a 'young writer who, for whatever reason, has not chosen to opt into Welsh' feels 'more separated from "Welshness" than his predecessors were because the shibboleth is now almost solely that of the language'. Cultural difference was not primarily built on a linguistic base for Mathias, but was rather embodied in a 'recognisably different lifestyle' that was being ignored and (to transpose J.R. Jones's metaphor to a different context) was disappearing beneath the young Anglo-Welsh writer's feet. 'Is Anglo-Welsh writing, in any meaningful sense of that term, likely to survive the century', asked Mathias in 1986.[8]

II

Contemporary critics, informed by European literary theory, might recognise the processes of losing the grounds of identity as 'deterritorialization', a concept defined and analysed by Gilles Deleuze and Felix Guattari in their volume *Kafka: Pour Une Littérature Mineure* (1975). Deleuze and Guattari argue, somewhat counter-intuitively, that 'minor literatures' are not written in minority languages. Minority languages share with majority languages a connection with a specific territory and assume a shared sense of ancestry and rootedness. The struggles of a minority language community, such as the Welsh-speaking community, will tend to involve making a claim for equality and recognition within a given territorial space, drawing on that same vertical interpenetration of language and territory deemed essential for national identity by J.R. Jones, and assumed to be the natural state of things by majority cultures. 'Minor literatures', for Deleuze and Guattari, are written in languages that may be dominant elsewhere but find themselves minoritized in a new context. 'Minor literature' is written in a language that has been removed from the ties of family, place and tradition and planted as a 'stranger in a strange land'. Their example is Kafka, the Jew from Prague writing German in a Czech city. German becomes 'deterritorialized' in a Czech context, especially so for 'the Prague Jews' who experience the 'feeling of an irreducible distance from their primitive Czech territoriality'. For them, German is 'deterritorialized' in a Czech setting, a language 'cut off from the masses, like a "paper language" or an artificial language' and the Jews are thus like 'gypsies who have stolen a German child from its crib.'

> In short, Prague German is a deterritorialized language, appropriate for strange and minor uses. (This can be compared in another context to what blacks in America today are able to do with the English language).[9]

Given their emphasis on writers who 'are simultaneously a part' of the minority culture 'and excluded from it' and their suggestion – in the reference to African American writers – of the wider applicability of their theory, it is perhaps not surprising that this theory of 'minor literature' by Deleuze and Guatarri has been adopted and adapted by several critics of Welsh writing in English.[10] Ian Gregson , for example, reads the Anglophone Welsh writer's situation as inherently deterritorialized. He argues that the relationship between 'language and homeland [...] is conspicuously denied the Welsh', and while this is a source of creative potential for many contemporary voices, it is a source of 'anger' for those who 'share the ideology of majoritarian thinkers' in assuming 'that a language and a homeland should be in a natural and universal relationship with each other'. Thus, argues Gregson, in the works of writers such as R.S. Thomas and Gillian Clarke this 'anger' results in a 'desperate, but inevitably frustrated, attempt to reterritorialize'.[11]

If Roland Mathias's cultural criticism challenges the linguistic nationalism of a Saunders Lewis in emphasising grounds other than language for identity, it also poses a challenge to the view of Welsh writing in English as an inherently 'deterritorialized' minor literature. The process being described in Mathias's conclusion to his *An Illustrated History* may be identified as 'deterritorialization', but that process is advancing in his description of it and is not therefore an inevitable state of affairs. Mathias's diagnosis of the Anglo-Welsh predicament assumes that a territorialized Anglo-Welshness existed before the 'old shibboleths' of 'Nonconformity and the closeness of the rural community' had begun to wane. Drawing on the terms of Gregson's analysis, there is little overt 'anger' in Mathias's writing, and rarely does he evoke a sense of desperation, but there is no doubting his desire to 'territorialize' English language literature in Wales. Language could not be the primary determinant of Welshness for Mathias, for he knew from his own experience of 'lifestyles' which were distinctively Welsh though articulated in English. The range of Mathias's critical activities, documented and described by Jane Aaron in the introduction, were designed precisely to forge the kind of rooted and venerable tradition for Anglo-Welsh literature claimed by territorialized cultures. Yet, as Aaron also notes, the vast majority of the writers who Mathias was excavating 'had largely been forgotten'.[12]

We may detect here a contradiction that informs Mathias's critical practice. For while he is analysing an Anglo-Welsh literary tradition, he is also simultaneously constructing it. Mathias is deploying the tools of the literary critic to explore a tradition and identify its formal and thematic characteristics, but is also bringing into being an invisible tradition that does not yet exist outside the critic's fertile mind; it has no material existence beyond the library stacks and does not yet exist in the popular nor the academic consciousness. There is a relationship, in this respect, between the literary critic and the minority nationalist; a desired 'tradition' or 'nation' is at once potentially in existence, and yet needs to be constructed; it is present and absent simultaneously, caught in a perpetual tension between actual and ideal.[13] Behind the activities of both lies a fear that Mathias seems to articulate in the opening quotation; what if, after the shibboleth has been uttered and the river crossed, one is faced with an absence, a desert? While the process of identifying a literary canon involves giving substance and material existence to a tradition, might it also be claimed that Welsh literary criticism, in both languages, is driven by an underlying fear of the revelation of nothing, of nowhere? This seems, in Mathias's analysis above, to be increasingly the fate of the

Anglo-Welsh as the 'old shibboleths' disappear, with the sole remaining shibboleth of the Welsh language itself in, potentially, an irreversible spiral of decline.

III

To read this anthology in these terms is to wonder whether there is anything distinctively Welsh about the poets collected between its covers? Rhian Edwards's Bridgend is a generalisable world of parents' evenings, pest controllers and Skype calls. Tiffany Atkinson's poems can often be located in Aberystwyth, but speak of plumbers, paperback romances and tourist beaches. Ailbhe Darcy writes postcards from Europe and offers two contrasting poetic responses to giving birth. The impression that theirs is a 'deterritorialized' poetry is appropriately reinforced by the Kafkaesque resonances of Darcy speaking of cockroaches, and Edwards describing a schoolgirl's story in which 'her father is a Beatle' (though it's probable that she has the band rather than the insect in mind).[14] Language also becomes deterritorialized and loses its moorings as Gwyneth Lewis traces the effects of dementia in the forgetting of the names for birds, noting that 'Words have migrated / I forget their calls', and while Philip Gross seeks a 'Heartland', it is a history of emigration – 'leaching families / out of their thin farms / to boats, to cities' – that he encounters in his pursuit of it.[15] On the whole, these poets move away from a single authorial voice, refuse the comforts of a coherent self, often emphasise fragments or foreground brokenness – in content, syntax and form – and adopt multiple viewpoints and colliding linguistic registers. They may be described as writing a poetry of 'elsewhere'. In this respect they seem to exemplify Matthew Jarvis's argument that contemporary post-devolution poetry in Wales tends towards individualism as opposed to communalism, towards 'dramas of the individual' as opposed to 'dramas of the state' or the nation.[16] While we might not wish to repeat Saunders Lewis's view of Dylan Thomas by arguing that this poetry 'belongs to the English', we might legitimately conclude that it belongs to a transnational Anglosphere. Are a number of the works contained in this anthology, then, the products of poets 'completely shut out from the Welsh world', producing the kind of poetry that Mathias feared in 1988? More broadly, might we argue that Wales, in the new millennium, has been undergoing, simultaneously, the seemingly contradictory processes of political devolution and cultural disembowelment?

For such arguments to be persuasive we would need a way of explaining why one should think that what people used to do, but no longer do, constitutes their 'real' identity, while what they actually do in the present does not. In what way can it be said that what former Welsh-speakers now English-speakers, former Nonconformists now atheists, former farmers now hedge-fund managers, have lost is their 'identity'? 'Insofar as our culture remains nothing more than what we do and believe, it is impotently descriptive' notes Walter Benn Michaels in a critique of contemporary cultural pluralism:

> The fact, in other words, that something belongs to our culture, cannot count as a motive for our doing it since, if it does belong to our culture we are already doing it, and if we don't do it (if we've stopped or haven't yet started doing it) it doesn't belong to our culture.[...] It is only if we think that our culture is not whatever beliefs and practices we actually happen to have but is instead the beliefs and practices that should properly go with the kind of people we happen to be that the fact of something belonging to our culture can count as a reason for doing it. But to think this is to appeal to something that must be beyond culture and that cannot be derived from culture precisely because our sense of which culture is properly ours must be derived from it.[17]

The poems collected in this anthology can be seen to veer between the two poles of Michaels's analysis; between culture as what 'we are already doing' on the one hand, and culture as the 'beliefs and practices that should properly go with the kind of people we happen to be' on the other. If Atkinson, Darcy and Edwards may be seen to exemplify the former, then Ruth

Bidgood and Christine Evans embody the latter.

Bidgood communicates a deep knowledge of a particular place and culture. Hers is poetry of roots and rootedness voiced by a lyric 'I' that shares this knowledge and imparts this sense of territorial locatedness. A land and its history form that 'something beyond culture', to which Benn Michaels refers, in the poetry of Ruth Bidgood as she leads us along a 'damp, richly green downward path' into

> a valley we knew,
> hills bare, hills forested, and far off,
> beyond misty lowlands, a horizon
> of true mountains.[18]

The view is 'new, aslant, changed' in the poem, but there is no doubting the speaker's knowledge and familiarity with this land as she identifies 'Big freestanding hawthorns [...] coming into bloom', and as

> oaks, ancient vegetable presences,
> sport young fern along branches,
> pallid fungi on trunks.[19]

Christine Evans shares this sense of interiority and identification with a particular landscape. A native of Yorkshire, hers is an elective Welshness informed by a profound knowledge of landscape and language that never wholly transcends the sympathetic outsider's awareness and respect for difference. This tension between interiority and exteriority, of being simultaneously territorialized and deterritorialized, is captured as the sense of rootedness evoked by sitting 'in a warm, walled garden/ on an island / at the extremity of a green peninsula' is undercut by reading about 'nomads'.[20] Abergwaun, Cernyw, Llydaw (Fishguard, Cornwall, Brittany) are identified by their Welsh names, indicating a Welsh-speaker's perspective on the world, though is seems that the process of cultural immersion results in the uncanny experience of feeling 'played to a tune /

I scarcely recognise'.[21] Evans asks us to consider whether there is a 'deeper dumbness' that language 'disguises'.[22] 'Deeper' suggests greater depth and interiority, while 'dumbness' (in keeping with my earlier analysis of the fear at the heart of Welsh cultural criticism) suggests silence and nothingness.

This tension between substance and absence, materiality and immateriality, is captured in Dannie Abse's sequence of poems on 'Hotel Nights'. Faced with the cultural 'desert' of his room at the 'Holiday Inn', complete with 'pyrexia of unknown origin', Abse turns to the symbols and practices of his Jewish ancestry, populating the space with the 'fiery furnace', 'David dancing before the Lord' and 'wise Solomon'.[23] The poem juxtaposes an idea of culture as what 'we are already doing' (staying in a Holiday Inn), and of culture as what we should be doing given 'the kind of people we happen to be' (drawing inspiration from the Hebrew Bible). While the effect is self-consciously comic, Abse is also taking us back to the Jewish sources of the shibboleth and the struggle for cultural survival. Abse writes a poetry 'trembling, awake with otherness', and the markers of cultural difference are not only Jewish, as the poems to Iolo Morganwg and, elsewhere in the same collection, to Dylan Thomas attest.[24] The view, shared by Saunders Lewis, Iorwerth Peate, Bobi Jones and others, that Anglo-Welsh writers had no distinctive tradition of their own and inevitably drew on English sources was resoundingly rejected by Roland Mathias.[25] Mathias's challenge to that view is supported in this anthology as Abse draws inspiration from Iolo Morganwg and John Freeman, in turn, writes a tribute to Dannie Abse thus continuing a 'conversation we had barely started'.[26] While Robert Minhinnick and Owen Sheers write war poems set, respectively, in Iraq and Afghanistan, *Pink Mist*'s epigraph from Aneirin's sixth century *Gododdin* indicates that the resonances and resources of a tradition – to which Wilfred Owen, David Jones and Alun Lewis may be legitimately said to belong – are being deployed in giving form and articulation to trauma and atrocity.

This anthology, then, suggests that the 'deterritorialization' that Deleuze and Guattari thought central to minor literature cannot be straightforwardly ascribed to literature written in a particular language or place. Contemporary Welsh poetry in English can range from the territorialized voice of Ruth Bidgood to the deterritorialized world of Tiffany Atkinson. This range also characterises the Welsh language tradition where the connection between language and land was powerfully expressed in the territorial poetry of Dic Jones and Gerallt Lloyd Owen, but was problematised and deterritorialized in the works of Alun Llewelyn Williams, say, writing in the primarily Anglophone world of mid-twentieth-century Cardiff.[27] The critic Simon Brooks has recently traced a tradition of deterritorialized voices who, from the Jewish-German Kate Bosse-Griffiths to the Geordie Toni Bianchi, retain a sense of otherness while writing through the medium of Welsh.[28] *Contra* Deleuze and Guattari, who map the distinction between territorial and deterritorial literatures onto the minoritisation of transplanted languages, the literatures of Wales suggest that we are dealing with a continuum, from territorial to deterritorial, that cuts across the binaries of Cymrophone and Anglophone, minority and majority.

IV

Roland Mathias challenged influential analyses of Welsh culture by insisting not only that Wales's Anglophone tradition had a venerable tradition and thus a claim to territorialization, but that – with the withering of cultural distinctiveness in the twentieth-century – it shared with Welsh language culture the 'experience of knowing, not that you are leaving your nation, but that your nation is leaving you, disappearing beneath your feet'. To what extent does this analysis remain relevant today? Against the potential of cultural dissolution evoked by Roland Mathias and J.R. Jones, an alternative narrative would emphasise the ways in which the process of establishing a political and civic frame for the nation has allowed a plurality of 'lifestyles' to flourish. While the story in The Book of Judges suggests that language might ultimately be at the core of cultural distinctiveness, we might argue that a healthy national culture is one that is plural in the articulations of its existence and difference, and thus offers a diversity of shibboleths as paths towards entry and acceptance. It would be a fitting last respect to Roland Mathias if this anthology of prizewinners functioned, for some of its readers, as a shibboleth leading to a crossing of the river towards further engagement with the literatures of Wales.

Notes

1. Roland Mathias, *Anglo-Welsh Literature: An Illustrated History* (Bridgend: Poetry Wales Press, 1987), p. 126.

2. The Book of Judges, 12: 5-6. The Bible: Authorized King James Version with Apocrypha (Oxford: Oxford University Press, 1997), p. 312.

3. See Marc Shell's discussion in *Stutter* (Cambridge MA: Harvard University Press, 2005), pp. 55-61. Tomos Owen draws on Jacques Derrida in his essay 'Shibboleth: For Dylan Thomas', in Kieron Smith and Rhian Barfoot (eds.), *New Theoretical Perspectives on Dylan Thomas* (Cardiff: University of Wales Press, 2020), pp.17–36.

4. Roland Mathias, *Complete Poems*. Edited by Sam Adams (Cardiff: University of Wales Press, 2002), p. 158.

5. Indicative examples can be found in David T. Lloyd, ed., *Writing on the Edge: Interviews with Writers and Editors of Wales* (Amsterdam: Rodopi, 1997).

6. Jane Aaron, 'Worth the Record', pp. 11-12.

7. J.R. Jones, *Gwaedd yng Nghymru* (Lerpwl: Cyhoeddiadau Modern Cymreig, 1970), 82; my translation. The original reads: 'Ond mi wn am brofiad arall sydd yr un mor ingol […] a hwnnw yw'r profiad o wybod, nid eich bod chwi yn gadael eich gwlad ond fod eich gwlad yn eich gadael chwi, yn darfod allan o fod o dan eich traed chwi, yn cael ei sugno i ffwrdd oddiwrthych, megis gan lyncwynt gwancus, i ddwylo ac i feddiant gwlad a gwareiddiad arall.'

8. Mathias, *Anglo-Welsh Literature*, p. 124.

9. Gilles Deleuze and Felix Guattari, *Kafka: Toward a Minor Literature*, trans. Dana Polan (Minneapolis: University of Minnesota Press, 1986), 16-17. 'Stranger in a stranger in a strange land' is from Exodus 2:22.

10. See, for example: Ian Gregson, *The New Poetry in Wales* (Cardiff: University of Wales Press, 2007); Laura Wainwright, *New Territories in Modernism: Anglophone Welsh Writing 1930-1949* (Cardiff: University of Wales Press, 2018).

11. Gregson, p. 3.

12. Aaron, 'Worth the Record', p. 14.

13. I'm influenced here by Slavoj Žižek's analysis of the 'future anterior' in his *Less Than Nothing: Hegel and the Shadow of Dialectical Materialism* (London: Verso, 2012) pp. 556-79. His emphasis is on the effect that generates its own cause, the utterance that produces its own intention, the subject that posits its own content.

14. Ailbhe Darcy, 'Nice', p. 131. Rhian Edwards, 'Parents Evening', p. 71.

15. Gwyneth Lewis, 'Field Guide to Dementia', p. 65. Philip Gross, 'Heartland', p. 102.

16. Matthew Jarvis, 'Repositioning Wales: Poetry after the Second Flowering', in Daniel G. Williams, ed., *Slanderous Tongues: Essays on Welsh Poetry in English 1970–2005* (Bridgend: Seren, 2010), p. 51.

17. Walter Benn Michaels, "Race into Culture: A Critical Genealogy of Cultural Identity" in Henry Louis Gates and K. Anthony Appiah, eds., *Identities* (Chicago: University of Chicago Press, 1995), p. 60.

18. Ruth Bidgood, 'Viewpoint', p. 49.

19. Bidgood, 'Lives', p. 52.

20. Christine Evans, 'Songline', p. 28.

21. Evans, Llŷn, p. 29. 'Unseen Island', p. 25.

22. Evans, 'Case History', p. 33.

23. Dannie Abse, 'In the Holiday Inn', p. 38.

24. Abse, 'North', p. 37. 'Iolo Morganwg', p. 41. 'Dylan' in *Running Late* (London: Hutchinson, 2006), p. 43.

25. See R.M. Jones, *Ysbryd y Cwlwm: Delwedd y Genedl yn ein Llenyddiaeth* (Caerdydd: Gwasg Prifysgol Cymru, 1998), pp. 395-421. Jones discusses Roland Mathias's literary criticism in this book.

26. Abse, 'Iolo Morganwg', p. 41. John Freeman, 'Dannie', p. 41.

27. Translations of works by these poets appear in Menna Elfyn and John Rowlands, eds., *The Bloodaxe Book of Modern Welsh Poetry* (Tarset: Bloodaxe, 2003).

50. Simon Brooks, 'Cymry Newydd a'u Llên', *Taliesin* 156 (2015), 33–42.

Biographical Notes

Jane Aaron (b. 1951)
Jane Aaron was Professor of English at the University of Glamorgan from 1999 until her retirement in 2011. She is now Emeritus Professor of English at the University of South Wales. She is noted for her work on the writings of Welsh women in both Welsh and English. As the author of *Nineteenth Century Women's Writing in Wales*, she won the Roland Mathias Prize in 2009. Her most recent works include *Welsh Gothic* (University of Wales Press, 2013) and (with Sarah Prescott), *Welsh Writing in English 1536-1914: The First Four Hundred Years* (Oxford University Press, 2020).

Christine Evans (b. 1943)
Born in Yorkshire, Christine Evans settled on the Llŷn Peninsula in the 1960s and still lives near Aberdaron. She married into a family which had farmed on the island of Bardsey (Ynys Enlli) for generations and she spends half of each year living there. She began writing poetry while on maternity leave in 1976, and the island features strongly in her work. *Selected Poems* is her seventh collection of poetry.
Roland Mathias Prize 2005 for *Selected Poems* (Seren)
Citation: "An impressive collection. Christine Evans has the ability to define and celebrate place and express a strong sense of continuity of human occupation."

Dannie Abse (1923-2014)
Born in Cardiff to Jewish parents, Dannie Abse studied medicine and worked in a chest clinic in London for more than thirty years. He maintained strong links with Wales, keeping a house in Ogmore-by-Sea. He produced some twenty volumes of verse, but, although best known as a poet, he wrote a number of prose works such as *The Presence* about life after the death of his wife Joan in a car crash.
Roland Mathias Prize 2007 for *Running Late* (Hutchinson)
Citation: "*Running Late* contains wonderful evocations of atmosphere, regret, longing for the simple, familiar things – and anticipation of it all passing."

Ruth Bidgood (b. 1922)

Born in Seven Sisters, Ruth Bidgood studied English at Oxford and worked as a coder in Egypt in World War Two. She has lived in mid-Wales since the 1960s when she moved to the tiny hamlet of Abergwesyn. She now lives in Beulah, a few miles away. She has published thirteen books of poetry, primarily about the landscapes and people of mid-Powys.

Roland Mathias Prize 2011 for *Time Being* (Seren)

Citation: "The crowning collection of her long career – she packs such an emotional punch. The quality of writing is sustained throughout and yet she makes it look so easy."

Gwyneth Lewis (b. 1959)

Gwyneth Lewis is one of the most prominent poets of her generation and was the first-ever National Poet of Wales appointed in 2005. She was bought up in Cardiff and writes in both Welsh and English. She has published nine collections of poetry and is also a dramatist, librettist and non-fiction writer. It was she who wrote the inscription on the face of the Wales Millennium Centre in Cardiff.

Roland Mathias Prize 2012 for *Sparrow Tree* (Bloodaxe Books)

Citation: "An outstanding talent for coining unexpected images from a range of sources, with her thoughts returning again and again to the many pains of absence and the suspenseful anticipation of loss."

Rhian Edwards (b. 1977)

Born in Bridgend, Rhian Edwards moved to Derbyshire and then London where she began working as a tax consultant. She soon became a singer, songwriter and full-time writer. She won the Roland Mathias Prize with her first collection of poetry. She is a prolific performer, winning the John Tripp Award for spoken poetry. Her latest collection, *The Estate Agents' Daughter*, was published in 2020.

Roland Mathias Prize and Wales Book of the Year 2013 for *Clueless Dogs* (Seren)

Citation: "A strikingly confident new voice. Full of verve and humour, her language has a winning intensity and honesty. She has an unerring ability to find the extraordinary in the ordinary."

Owen Sheers (b. 1974)

Owen Sheers is a poet, novelist and playwright who lives in Talgarth,

Powys. He has published novels such as *Resistance*, which was made into a film, plays such as *Mametz* based on a battle in World War I, and collections of poetry such as *Skirrid Hill*. *Pink Mist*, of which one extract has been selected, is a verse drama about modern warfare seen through the eyes of soldiers serving in Afghanistan and their families at home. Owen Sheers is currently Professor of Creativity at Swansea University.

Roland Mathias Prize and Wales Book of the Year 2014 for *Pink Mist* (Faber)

Citation: "This is a powerful work of great emotional intensity. He conveys the reality of war for these young men – and the impact particularly on the women in their families – in a way which at times is intensely moving."

Tiffany Atkinson (b. 1972)

Born in Berlin to an army family, Tiffany Atkinson moved to Wales in 1993, becoming a lecturer at Aberystwyth University. She has won a number of awards for her poetry, and *So Many Moving Parts*, which depicts the awkward relationship between body and spirit, was her third collection to be published. A fourth, *Lumen*, was published in 2021. She is currently Professor of Creative Writing at the University of East Anglia.

Roland Mathias Prize 2015 for *So Many Moving Parts* (Bloodaxe Books)

Citation: "One of Britain's best contemporary poets who has produced poems which always surprise and which force the reader to engage. It is the juxtaposition of different events, ideas or feelings which catch the reader".

Philip Gross (b. 1952)

Born in Cornwall, Philip Gross moved to Wales in 2004 to become Professor of Creative Writing at the University of Glamorgan. He has published more than twenty volumes of poetry and won several major awards such as the T.S. Eliot Prize for his collection *The Water Table*. His latest collection is *Between the Islands*, published in 2020. He is well-known for his readings, which he regards as more of a conversation than a performance. He is also a prolific novelist for young people.

Roland Mathias Prize 2016 for *Love Songs of Carbon* (Bloodaxe Books)

Citation: "He writes with a full-throated clarity that sounds, suddenly, like no-one else around. Some of his poems here are tantamount to love poems, not just to the person but the body itself."

John Freeman (b. 1946)
Born in Essex, John Freeman was brought up in South London and studied English at Cambridge. He lived in Yorkshire before moving to Wales to teach English at Cardiff University. *What Possessed Me* was his tenth collection of poems and he has also published a collection of essays entitled *The Less Received: Neglected Modern Poets*. He lives near Cowbridge in the Vale of Glamorgan.
Roland Mathias Prize 2017 for *What Possessed Me* (Worple Press)
Citation: "A brilliant, witty, charming, accessible, and above all moving, collection of poems about family, about place and about the past."

Robert Minhinnick (b. 1952)
Born in Neath, Robert Minhinnick is a poet, novelist, essayist and environmental campaigner. He co-founded Friends of the Earth Cymru in 1984 and the cause is reflected in much of his writing, including *Diary of the Last Man*. He was editor of *Poetry Wales* between 1997 and 2008, and has published seven collections of poetry as well as several essay collections and novels. His work deals with Welsh and international themes and he has won the Wales Book of the Year a record three times. He lives in Porthcawl.
Roland Mathias Prize and Wales Book of the Year 2018 for *Diary of the Last Man* (Carcanet)
Citation: "A serious book for serious times, reflecting above all the poets' ecological and political concerns. The elegiac and melancholic themes are perfectly balanced by the poet's indefatigable drive towards the rendering of beauty, most particularly that of the natural world."

Ailbhe Darcy (b. 1981)
Born and brought up in Dublin, Ailbhe Darcy now lives in Cardiff where she is a Senior Lecturer in Creative Writing at Cardiff University. She has spent several years studying and teaching in the American rustbelt, which informs much of her second collection of poetry, *Insistence*. She now regards herself as a Welsh as well as an Irish poet.
Roland Mathias Prize and Wales Book of the Year 2019 for *Insistence* (Bloodaxe Books)

Citation: "Darcy's *Insistence* plumbs the darkness of vulnerability in a world proliferating with danger. Her poems marvel at the borders of selfhood with an unflinching courage."

The Editors

Glyn Mathias (b. 1945)

Glyn Mathias OBE has more than 30 years' experience in journalism, becoming Political Editor for ITN and then for BBC Wales. He subsequently served as the first Electoral Commissioner for Wales and as the Welsh Member on the Ofcom Content Board in London. His autobiography, *Raising an Echo*, was published in 2014. He was Chair of the Roland Mathias Prize Committee and is President of the Brecknock Society and Museum Friends.

Daniel G. Williams (b. 1972)

Daniel G. Williams is Professor of English and is Director of the Richard Burton Centre for the Study of Wales at Swansea University. His publications include *Ethnicity and Cultural Authority: From Arnold to Du Bois* (Edinburgh University Pres, 2006), *Black Skin, Blue Books: African Americans and Wales* (University of Wales Press, 2012) and *Wales Unchained: Literature, Politics and Identity in the American Century* (University of Wales Press, 2015).

Acknowledgements

Selected Poems by Christine Evans (2004)
Time Being by Ruth Bidgood (2009)
Clueless Dogs by Rhian Edwards (2012)
Reproduced by permission of Seren Books www.serenbooks.com

Sparrow Tree by Gwyneth Lewis (2011)
So Many Moving Parts by Tiffany Atkinson (2014)
Love Songs of Carbon by Philip Gross (2015)
Insistence by Ailbhe Darcy (2018)
Reproduced by permission of Bloodaxe Books www.bloodaxe-books.com

Running Late by Dannie Abse (2006), published by Hutchinson www.penguin.co.uk
Reproduced by permission of United Agents, 12-26 Lexington Street, London W1F 0LE

Pink Mist by Owen Sheers (2012), published by Faber & Faber (www.faber.co.uk)
Reproduced by permission of the author c/o Rogers, Coleridge & White Ltd., 20 Powis Mews, London W11 1JN

What Possessed Me by John Freeman (2016)
Reproduced by permission of Worple Press www.worplepress.com

Diary of the Last Man by Robert Mininnick (2017)
Reproduced by permission of Carcanet Press www.carcanet.co.uk

A Last Respect

Roland Mathias (1915-2007)

The sun, disinterested, summer on either side
Of the watershed, glanced along every road
In the county. It was a weather just
For a last progress, a proportion of death
In the hazels' cardust and the early yellowing
Of the lake trees, of life too, tetchy and pale
In the blown colts that the cold cliff of winter
Would rear into stallions. The processional cars
Had sound, yes, but a small sound like dust
Dropping on dust and the rush of hedgerows
Touched and not touched, a sound like a sigh
Caught in the tunnel of hazels and falling
Back, wheel by wheel, bowing and hollowing
Towards the minor hierarchies of grief.
It was July: there was no want of leaf.
Flowers the shire over were not hard to come by.

The lane was south. Above Cantref hazed green
Shoulders held up the farther points, the pinnacles
Of Sion, and their shimmer was an eye
Over the dying world, a blood that the dead
Plead by and pilgrims when they wake.
The settled dust on the hazels looked less grey
Than the new dust raised as the wheeling drift held on
Slowly towards those mountains, no move
Of mouth or limb. Sure as the heart empties
The last thick syllables dissuade the tongue.

In this hiatus when no stolid ghost respires
All that was left of breath suddenly ruffed the flowers
On the bier ahead. The hearse, its guttural base,

Ground into some declivity of gear and all
But the elm and the brass handles had air
About it and petals flying, impassioned as
Wings, an arc of will prescribed, mounting
And Sion crying, quick in the eyelash second.

Who are you to say that my father, wily
And old in the faith, had not in that windflash abandoned
His fallen minister's face?